Quod scriptura, non iubet vetat

The Latin translates, "What is not commanded in scripture, is forbidden:'

On the Cover: Baptists rejoice to hold in common with other evangelicals the main principles of the orthodox Christian faith. However, there are points of difference and these differences are significant. In fact, because these differences arise out of God's revealed will, they are of vital importance. Hence, the barriers of separation between Baptists and others can hardly be considered a trifling matter. To suppose that Baptists are kept apart solely by their views on Baptism or the Lord's Supper is a regrettable misunderstanding. Baptists hold views which distinguish them from Catholics, Congregationalists, Episcopalians, Lutherans, Methodists, Pentecostals, and Presbyterians, and the differences are so great as not only to justify, but to demand, the separate denominational existence of Baptists. Some people think Baptists ought not teach and emphasize their differences but as E.J. Forrester stated in 1893, "Any denomination that has views which justify its separate existence, is bound to promulgate those views. If those views are of sufficient importance to justify a separate existence, they are important enough to create a duty for their promulgation ... the very same reasons which justify the separate existence of any denomination make it the duty of that denomination to teach the distinctive doctrines upon which its separate existence rests." If Baptists have a right to a separate denominational life, it is their duty to propagate their distinctive principles, without which their separate life cannot be justified or maintained.

Many among today's professing Baptists have an agenda to revise the Baptist distinctives and redefine what it means to be a Baptist. Others don't understand why it even matters. The books being reproduced in the *Baptist Distinctives Series* are republished in order that Baptists from the past may state, explain and defend the primary Baptist distinctives as they understood them. It is hoped that this Series will provide a more thorough historical perspective on what it means to be distinctively Baptist.

The Lord Jesus Christ asked, *"And why call ye me, Lord, Lord, and do not the things which I say?"* (Luke 6:46). The immediate context surrounding this question explains what it means to be a true disciple of Christ. Addressing the same issue, Christ's question is meant to show that a confession of discipleship to the Lord Jesus Christ is inconsistent and untrue if it is not accompanied with a corresponding submission to His authoritative commands. Christ's question teaches us that a true recognition of His authority as Lord inevitably includes a submission to the authority of His Word. Hence, with this question Christ has made it forever impossible to separate His authority as King from the authority of His Word. These two principles—the authority of Christ as King and the authority of His Word—are the two most fundamental Baptist distinctives. The first gives rise to the second and out of these two all the other Baptist distinctives emanate. As F.M. Iams wrote in 1894, "Loyalty to Christ as King, manifesting itself in a constant and unswerving obedience to His will as revealed in His written Word, is the real source of all the Baptist distinctives:' In the search for the *primary* Baptist distinctive many have settled on the Lordship of Christ as the most basic distinctive. Strangely, in doing this, some have attempted to separate Christ's Lordship from the authority of Scripture, as if you could embrace Christ's authority without submitting to what He commanded. However, while Christ's Lordship and Kingly authority can be isolated and considered essentially for discussion's sake, we see from Christ's own words in Luke 6:46 that His Lordship is really inseparable from His Word and, with regard to real Christian discipleship, there can be no practical submission to the one without a practical submission to the other.

In the symbol above the Kingly Crown and the Open Bible represent the inseparable truths of Christ's Kingly and Biblical authority. The Crown and Bible graphics are supplemented by three Bible verses (Ecclesiastes 8:4, Matthew 28:18-20, and Luke 6:46) that reiterate and reinforce the inextricable connection between the authority of Christ as King and the authority of His Word. The truths symbolized by these components are further emphasized by the Latin quotation - *quod scriptura, non iubet vetat*— i.e., "What is not commanded in scripture, is forbidden:' This Latin quote has been considered historically as a summary statement of the regulative principle of Scripture. Together these various symbolic components converge to exhibit the two most foundational Baptist Distinctives out of which all the other Baptist Distinctives arise. Consequently, we have chosen this composite symbol as a logo to represent the primary truths set forth in the *Baptist Distinctives Series*.

A
DEFENCE
OF
"BAPTISM A TERM OF COMMUNION"

JOSEPH KINGHORN
1766-1832

Photo courtesy of:
Southern Baptist Historical Library and Archives,
Nashville, Tennessee

A
DEFENCE

OF

"BAPTISM A TERM OF COMMUNION"

IN ANSWER TO THE

REV. ROBERT HALL'S REPLY:

BY JOSEPH KINGHORN.

With a Biographical Sketch of the Author by John Franklin Jones

---

"AMONG ALL THE ABSURDITIES THAT EVER WERE HELD, NONE EVER MAINTAINED *THAT,* THAT ANY PERSON SHOULD PARTAKE OF THE COMMUNION BEFORE HE WAS BAPTISED." —WALL; History of Infant Baptism.

NORWICH:
PUBLISHED BY WILKIN AND YOUNGMAN, MARKET PLACE:
BY BALDWIN, CRADDOCK AND JOY, PATTERNOSTER ROW, LONDON;
AND BY WAUGH AND INNES, EDINBURGH
1820.

he Baptist Standard Bearer, Inc.
NUMBER ONE IRON OAKS DRIVE • PARIS, ARKANSAS 72855

Thou hast given a *standard* to them that fear thee;
that it may be displayed because of the truth.
– *Psalm 60:4*

Reprinted 2006

by

THE BAPTIST STANDARD BEARER, INC.
No. 1 Iron Oaks Drive
Paris, Arkansas 72855
(479) 963-3831

THE WALDENSIAN EMBLEM
lux lucet in tenebris
"The Light Shineth in the Darkness"

ISBN# 1579786324

CONTENTS.

PREFACE .... *Page* ix

CHAPTER I.
Introductory Observations 1

CHAPTER II.
On the Statement of the Controversy 19

CHAPTER III.
Mr. Hall's Reasonings, in the second and third chapters of his Reply, examined 33

SECTION I.—Statement of the Principle on which the present discussion depends,—Mr. Hall's arguments respecting our Lord's Commission examined 33

SECTION II.—Mr. Hall's arguments respecting Apostolic Precedent, examined 42

SECTION III.—Mr. Hall's assertion that we assume infallibility, examined and repelled 50

SECTION IV.—Mr. Hall's concessions:—his attempt to make the Apostles parties against us 55

SECTION V.—Mr. Hall's misrepresentation of the statement, that Baptism is a term of christian profession, exposed 59

SECTION VI.—The difference of sentiment among christians respecting the doctrine of Election—the prohibition to eat blood—and the imposition of hands on the baptised—examined as to their supposed bearing on this controversy 74

SECTION VII.—Mr. Hall's criticisms on the use of the term "evidence" examined—He does not recognise the scriptural design of baptism; and his system subverts the institution 82

CHAPTER IV.

An examination of Mr. Hall's third chapter on the connection between the two positive institutes 92

SECTION I.—His statement of the question examined;—his reasoning refuted 92

SECTION II.—Mistakes of Mr. Hall respecting Mr. Fuller—the Unities, Eph. iv.—and, Dr. Whitby.. 99

SECTION III.—Mr. Hall's reasoning concerning positive law and prohibition, examined 105

SECTION IV.—Mr. Hall's evasion of the argument on the connection of the two ordinances—his accusations confronted—his mistakes concerning the "Scottish Baptists", &c. 109

SECTION V.—A Review of the general subject:—the amount of Mr. Hall's argument:—the advantage he gives to the Pædobaptists:—recapitulation of what has been conceded and proved:—consequences resulting from our author's system 127

CHAPTER V.

On Dispensing with a christian ordinance............... 132

CHAPTER VI.

Mr. Hall's misrepresentations of the argument respecting the ground of dissent exposed 144

CHAPTER VII.

The Pædobaptists necessarily parties in the present controversy 157

CHAPTER VIII.

The scripture injunction respecting forbearance examined ... 164

CHAPTER IX.

Mr. Hall's argument for communing with Pædobaptists, because they are part of the true church, examined 183

CHAPTER X.

The charge of excluding, excommunicating, and punishing other denominations, considered 188

CHAPTER XI.

Mixed Communion unknown in the ancient church 193

CHAPTER XII.

Conclusion 199

PREFACE.

Although controversy has often been productive of many evils, and has given great reason for humiliation before God, yet it is frequently unavoidable, and we are indebted to it for a large portion of important information. It is a very remarkable expression of the Apostle Paul, when speaking of the different opinions which existed in the church of Corinth, "there must be also heresies among you, that they which are approved may be made manifest among you." (1 Cor. xi. 19.) The departure of some from the faith once delivered to the Saints, tried others, and shewed who were, and who were not willing to adhere to the doctrine of the Apostles; and those who did adhere to the truth in its simplicity, were compelled to contend for it with earnestness and vigour. When apostacy from the faith of the Gospel had become general, every attempt to bring men to a just view of the will of the Lord occasioned opposition and controversy, so that when the Reformers began the great work of turning men's attention to the truth as it is in Jesus, they were obliged in the first place to establish the supreme authority of the New Testament. When the Baptists came forth from the obscurity in which they, in common with other protestants, had been concealed, they had to contend in the same field in the midst of difficulties peculiarly severe. They called the attention of the world to what they considered a nearer approach to apostolic truth than other protestants had admitted; and they found enemies in the very men, who, in opposition to the Roman Catholics, pleaded for conformity to New Testament doctrine, and for the ordinances of the Gospel as practised in the apostolic church. They were esteemed *Heretics* by all parties; they were induced by their hard circumstances to study the New Testament closely, and to suspect the truth of many sentiments which were generally received without suspicion. Hence they were led to mark the difference between the church of Christ as *he* formed it, and a church established by the power of the state; and from this investigation they caught the first glimpse of that important principle of RELIGIOUS LIBERTY which it was their honour to bring forward to notice, and to defend in the midst of censure and obloquy.

The source of their sorrows, and the cause of their success, was their view of BAPTISM. Deriving their opinion from the New Testament, and appealing to that volume in their own defence, they found themselves fortified beyond the power of successful attack, because they could prove that they did no more than obey its injunctions. In doing what Christ commanded they were sure that they were acting rightly, and they were satisfied that their opponents could not bring equal evidence in favour of sentiments and practices which were neither enjoined by Jesus Christ, nor illustrated by the example of the apostolic church.

Like those who of old were zealous in building the temple of the Lord, they and their fellows were men wondered at. (*Zech.* iii. 8.) All the expedients which persecuting rage, scorn, bitterness, and misrepresentation could devise, were employed to sink them in public estimation, and to run them down as a despicable party, who were neither supported by truth, nor possessed of the talents and literature necessary for their own defence.

How vain is the storm that is raised by passion! When "a great and strong wind passed by, and rent the mountains, and broke in pieces the rocks before the Lord,—the Lord was not in the wind." (1 *Kings* xix. 11.) DR. FEATLY, a man of talent, of learning, and of considerable popularity in his day, took up his pen against the *Anabaptists*, and gratified himself by abusing them. He was honest enough to confess that he could hardly dip his pen "into any other liquor than the juice of gall"; but if he had not made this confession, his book was a sufficient evidence of his temper. His work was so popular that it passed through six editions in as many years; and doubtless many would think, that between his arguments, his literature, and his severity, the Baptists would be so overpowered, that they would never raise their heads again. The contrary, however, was the fact: "the more" their opponents "afflicted them, the more they multiplied and grew"; and could DR. FEATLY now rise from his grave, he would find them increased beyond his greatest apprehensions, and have the mortification of hearing that they bought his book as a curiosity, on account of its virulence, and often amused themselves by observing the violent explosions of his temper.

A specimen of a better kind was exhibited by MR. FLAVEL, a man of a different spirit, but still quite opponent to the *Anabaptists*. MR. PHILIP CARY, a Baptist minister at *Dartmouth*, had published a book on baptism, entitled, '*A Solemn Call*'; FLAVEL thought well of the author, yet he deemed it necessary to reply to his work. He treated him, however, respectfully, and appears to have been very desirous of not *misrepresenting* him. But it is curious to observe how he intreats him to consider the situation in which he had placed himself by venturing to plead the cause of '*Anabaptism*'. "As for your pretended solutions of the *incomparable* MR. BAXTER's, and the *learned* and *accurate* DR. BURTHOGGE's arguments, I admire at your confidence therein.——Alas! my friend, you little know what it is to have such weak and inartificial discourses as yours, brought under the strict *examen* of such acute and judicious eyes."* Between two such millstones, poor *Philip Cary* was doubtless to be ground to powder. Some things, however, resist all attacks, and in their nature are too hard to be crushed by human power. *Mr. Cary's* sentiment still continues to make its appeal to men on the ground of the New Testament representations, and spreads more and more: the reason is manifest, it is to be found in that sacred volume, and is supported by it. There it is seen that those only who believed in Christ were baptised; and that neither precept nor precedent can be discovered in favour of the administration of baptism to persons of any other description.

The debate which engages our attention at present, does not lead us to inquire either into the mode or subjects of baptism, but it directs our regard to a question which in point of importance takes the precedence of every other in the baptismal controversy; which is, whether baptism is an ordinance to be maintained in the church; or, whether it is one of those indifferent and unimportant things which the church has no right to consider as requisite to communion? Time alone can discover what will be the effect of the attempts now made, to justify the introduction of persons *professedly unbaptised.* We may be upon the verge of a new system of corruption, and may see the most unscriptural propositions and practices become popular: but so long as the New

---

* Flavel's Works, vol. viii. p. 202. Ed. 8vo. 1770.

Testament is acknowledged to be the source of authority, we shall say to those who adopt the theory of Mr. Hall, as we do to our friends, who plead for infant baptism;—go to the scriptures and *find it there*, and then we shall be satisfied.

We do not intend to rest the argument on *expediency*, but as Mr. Hall brought forward this consideration himself (though he blamed us for the notice we took of it), it may not be amiss to mention a few facts which our forefathers have preserved, and which shew what was the tendency of the system of mixed communion in their day.

Every one acquainted in any degree with Nonconformist History, has often met with the name of Mr. John Tombes, who strenuously pleaded the cause of the baptists in his day, and by this means, was of eminent service to the body at large: but he held this sentiment, and his conduct shewed its tendency; for though after the act of uniformity had passed, he did not choose to conform and hold a living in the Establishment, yet he not only frequented the church of England, but actually *died in. her communion*, and thus his conduct tended to neutralize his arguments.

Mr. Baxter informs us of two "Anabaptists", (as he calls them) who were induced by his arguments and persuasion to adopt the plan of mixed communion; he says they both "*turned from anabaptistry and separation*"; and he adds, that "in sense of their old error," they "ran into the other extreme".*

The eminent JOHN BUNYAN, who zealously advocated the cause of mixed communion, seems to have had no great success in promoting the interests of the Baptists. We hardly ever find an allusion to the ordinance of baptism in his works, except in his controversial pieces, in which he practically undermines its authority. Nor was the effect of his favourite system conducive to the spread of his opinion as a baptist; for such was the state of the church with which he was long connected, that on his death they chose a Pædobaptist; and from the year 1688, in which he died, to the year 1788, when MR. JOSHUA SYMONDS died, the ministers who succeeded him were *Pædobaptists*, except the last, who some years after his settlement with the church, changed his sentiments and became a Baptist. This took place in 1772; but though MR. SYMONDS continued at Bedford, it was ' on the conditions that he should not introduce the controversy into the pulpit, nor into conversation, unless it was first mentioned by others.' We have also been informed, that one instance occurred in the year 1700, and another in 1724, in which the church refused to grant a dismission to members who desired to unite with two Baptist churches in London, because they were *strict communion* churches.

* See his Life and Times, by SYLVESTER, pt. ii. p. 180, and pt. iii. p. 180. The two persons were, MR. THOS. LAMB and MR. W. ALLEN; the general fact of their change of sentiment on this subject is confirmed by DANVERS in the postscript to his ' *Treatise of Baptism*', p. 53, 54.

DR. JAMES FOSTER, who was more than twenty years pastor of the General Baptist church in Barbican, London, and who in his day advocated the cause of mixed communion, left the General Baptists, and accepted the pastoral charge of the Independent church at Pinner's Hall, London. But, though he had pleaded the *expedience* of mixed communion as the means of leading men to consider what the Baptists had to urge in defence of their sentiments, yet Mr. GRANTHAM KILLINGWORTH informs us, that in conversation with him upon the point, " he could not pretend to say, that one single person who was in communion at Pinner's Hall before his going over to them, had since submitted to that institution, [of baptism] or shewn the least inclination to be baptised".*

The instances above recited mark the tendency of the system in times now considerably distant; at a later period MR. BOOTH shews what was *his* view of its tendency, and his manner of expression clearly evinces that he drew his remarks from *facts*. He says, " I would also take the liberty here to observe, that some of those churches in which free communion has been practised, have not been the most remarkable for brotherly love, or christian peace and harmony. Has the pastor of a church so constituted, being a Baptist, never found, that his Pædobaptist brethren have been a little offended, when he has ventured freely to speak his mind on the mode and subject of

* Killingworth's Answer to the Defence of Dr. Foster's Sermon of Catholic Communion, p. 35.

baptism? When Pædobaptist candidates for communion have been proposed to such a church, have those members who espoused the same sentiment never discovered a degree of pleasure, in the thought of having their number and influence increased in the community, that has excited the jealousy of their Baptist brethren? When, on the contrary, there has been a considerable addition to the number of Baptist members, has not an equal degree of pleasure in them, raised similar suspicions in the minds of their Pædobaptist brethren? And are not suspicions and jealousies of this kind, the natural effects of such a constitution?" *(Apol. p.* 131, 132.) No one who is acquainted with the character of ABRAHAM BOOTH, will for a moment suppose that he was writing from imagination: his concluding observation also, is too forcible to be denied:—" now, as our opponents must allow, that their communities are liable to all those other imperfections which are common to the churches of Christ; so, I presume, the reader will hardly forbear concluding, that free communion exposes them to some *additional* disadvantages, which are peculiar to themselves."*

One effect it will always produce; it will *exclude* those who think that the primitive constitution of the church ought to be preserved; and invite those who for any reason are opponent, either to baptism as an ordinance of Christ, or, to the form and order of the christian church as it

---

* Some observations on the experience of the American Baptist churches, the reader will meet with in the progress of the work.

was established by the Lord. Whether they come as persons baptised, or the contrary, they are equally accepted, and those who receive them practically declare, that though our view of baptism is justified by "overwhelming evidence," yet it does not now hold the situation in which it was placed by Jesus Christ. To us this consideration forms an unanswerable objection to the scheme: it eventually strikes at the *permanency* of the institution of the Lord; and no acuteness that has yet been brought into the discussion, can prove that it needs be regarded at all, if Mr. Hall's principles are admitted.

An anonymous author has lately shewn the tendency of these principles in an indirect but marked manner, in a pamphlet entitled, "*Thoughts on Baptism as an Ordinance of Proselytism, including observations on the controversy respecting terms of Communion; by Agnostos.*" This writer is the opponent of all parties, for his sentiment is, that if baptism was designed to be a standing ordinance of the church, *Missionaries* are the only proper administrators, and their proselytes the only proper subjects. Hence it follows, on his plan, that Baptists and Pædobaptists are equally wrong, and if his theory were admitted, the controversy respecting communion would immediately terminate. With his sentiments, it is to be expected that he would treat the principle of strict communion as a mistake; and that practically, he would be on the side of Mr. Hall: yet so far as the tendency of the sentiment is concerned, he throws his weight into the opposite scale. He observes justly,—"what can be more inconsistent than to maintain that Baptism is a positive institution and a standing ordinance of the christian church, and yet treat it as a matter of indifference and countenance the total neglect of it, by admitting to an *equal* participation of *all* the privileges of church fellowship those who are unbaptised, with those who have paid a regard to that ordinance?" *(p.* 109.) The controversy he calls "a contest between *Christian* principles and *Baptist* principles"; and he says either the law of baptism must be sacrificed, or the spirit of the Gospel of Christ must be violated". *(p.* 101.) According to this statement, what the author calls *christian* principles, cannot admit that our Lord appointed a positive rite to be obeyed, when his disciples enter on a public profession of his Gospel.— This, however, he must be aware, we should call an assumption; but if what he calls "*Baptist* principles" are supported by the New Testament, "*Christian* principles" will never be in opposition to *Christian institutions*. It is, therefore, only needful to shew that "*Baptist* principles" are *scriptural*, and then the subject is at rest, till it is proved to be also scriptural that we should form a church of persons *unbaptised*.

It is no part of our business to enter the lists with "Agnostos" respecting his main argument, but his observations on the tendency of mixed communion deserve the more attention as they proceed from a writer who was not led to make them from any partiality to the cause we are advocating. He grants that the objections urged against Mr. Hall's system are well founded; that in proportion as it prevails, the cause of the Baptists must sink; *(p.* 112.) that the effect of mixed communion, instead of inducing Pædobaptists to become Baptists, will tend in the contrary direction, and what they see and hear, will confirm them in their former ideas, that Baptism is of little or no importance, and altogether unnecessary. *(p.* 114.) Besides, he observes that where Baptists and Pædobaptists are indiscriminately associated, " it is generally *understood*, if not *absolutely stipulated*, as a term of communion, that *baptism should be kept out of sight as much as possible*; that it should *scarcely ever be mentioned*, and *never* be insisted on, lest the peace of the church should be disturbed, and the harmony of its members be interrupted." *(p.* 114, 115.) Farther, he observes, it exposes a minister to the temptation of shunning to declare the whole counsel of God in order to avoid giving offence; and it accustoms the people to see an *acknowledged duty* treated as a matter of indifference. And—it has a tendency to excite a spirit of jealousy between the two parties, destructive of peace and unity, and thus, he observes, one of the strongest arguments in favour of mixed communion is turned against the practice. *(p.* 117.)

The tendency of Mr. Hall's reasoning is also marked by a writer of a different description, who asks him *how he can justify his* DISSENT *from the church of England*, on the principles of his own work? THE REV. CHARLES JERRAM, *Vicar of Chobham*, in a volume entitled, "Conversations on Infant Baptism, and some popular objections against the Church of the United Kingdom," brings the subject forward in a long note. *(p.* 152, &c.) He classes Dr. Mason and Mr. Hall together; he compliments them both, and is glad that he can appeal to such unexceptionable authorities. He argues from what they have each brought forward; and contends that on their principles, Dissenters ought not to have left the Establishment. He observes, that Mr. Hall challenges the Baptists to produce a single instance of withdrawing from the ancient church on the account of Infant baptism;—that this shews at least the sentiment of *Mr. Hall*, that difference of opinion on this important rite, a difference so great as to ANNUL the ordinance in the minds of the Baptists, is not a legitimate cause of separation.—That if any thing may be considered as of such minor importance, that it may be merged for the sake of peace, the circumstantials in the administration of the Lord's supper may be viewed in that light; and he tells us that "the doctrine which Mr. Hall lays down as the foundation of a more extended communion among the various denominations of christians would *undoubtedly lead to this conclusion.*"—That "we have the authority of Mr. Hall for asserting, that nothing less than a radical defection from the purity of apostolical doctrine and discipline can authorise the principle of separation or exclusion from christian communion." This Mr. Jerram says is, "*a most important concession*"! and he adds,—" we may challenge the world to substantiate such a charge against us, as would render it improper, on *these principles*, to continue within her pale, or make it a matter of indifference to desert her community." *(p.*160.162.)

The reasoning that can dispose of an institution of Christ, by removing it from its primitive station, introduces so lax a principle, that no precept which we do not consider essential to salvation, can maintain its ground. If we are not bound to adhere to a positive appointment of Christ, which is confessedly permanent in its obligation, we in vain assert, that it is of consequence to form the church according to the plan which Christ has furnished; for it may always be retorted, what avails your pleading scripture, when you reason away the authority of one of its plainest institutes? Mr. Jerram is a man of sense, he sees the advantage which is given him, and we doubt not he will use it.

But it is time to conclude this long preface. I have now discharged a duty which I owed to the denomination of which I am an unworthy member; and I commit the following pages to the reader's attention, asking for nothing more, than that he will consider how far the observations he may meet with, agree with the New Testament. Should he accuse me of repeating the same arguments in different parts of the work, my apology is, that it arose from following the detail of Mr. Hall's reasonings, which, in my apprehension, were continually in opposition to a few plain principles by which the controversy must eventually be decided. Repetition was therefore (to a degree at least) unavoidable, unless I had adopted a totally different plan, which would have been open to the the objection, that I had not examined my opponent's arguments in their order. As my attention has been awakened to this subject by a variety of circumstances, I shall listen to any *fair* and *candid* argument which may yet be presented from any quarter; but unless something should be urged, far superior to any thing that has yet appeared, it is not likely that I shall trouble the world with a reply. Contention is not desirable; but, if we are not willing tamely to surrender the cause of truth, it is sometimes unavoidable. In pleading for what I believe is the will of the Lord, I hope that I earnestly desire to keep an eye on his character and glory, while I intreat his forgiveness of my weakness and imperfections in this attempt to direct the attention of professing christians to the *ordinances* of the Gospel, as Christ and his Apostles *delivered them unto us.*

NORWICH,
September, 1820.

CHAPTER I.

INTRODUCTORY OBSERVATIONS.

THE controversy respecting Terms of Communion has various bearings on subjects not immediately connected with the original question. A disposition minutely to examine the principles on which Dissenting churches ought to proceed in the regulation of their internal concerns, has of late been very manifest; and, we trust, the investigation will promote the cause of truth. They who plead for nothing more than what they find in the New Testament, need not fear the result of the inquiry, so long as that volume is preserved entire, and is freely circulated for the use of the Church.

If then, in the progress of the examination, it is asked, on what terms persons were admitted into the Church in apostolic times, and what was the platform of the primitive discipline; we reply, the New Testament informs us, that he who professed faith in Christ, and whose profession was considered worthy of credit, was baptised, and then took his place in the assembly of the faithful as one who had "put on Christ." So long as he filled up the various duties to which God had called him, it does not appear that he was subjected to further examination, or required to renew his profession. It was taken for granted, that he who continued to walk in the ways of the Lord, was acting on the principles he had already professed. If he changed his residence, and went where he was not known, "letters of commendation" were an introduction to other churches, on the ground of which, the stranger was received, and treated as a brother. If, however, in any period of his profession, he deviated from the path of duty, he was warned and admonished; if his conduct rendered further severity needful, he was excluded; but if he repented and turned again to the Lord, he was again admitted to the privileges of Communion.

The directions which the New Testament gives us on this subject, relate only to the great points which should ever be kept in view; and not to those minutiæ for which no general rule could make provision. It was necessary that the question, "dost thou believe on the Son of God?" should be answered; and the church had a right to expect, that whoever wished to unite with them, would be "ready to give a reason of the hope that was in him with meekness and fear:" but the mode of making such a profession is left undetermined. Whatever relates to particulars concerning which we have no rule given, is fairly open to examination, and if needful, to alteration. We ought to take care lest by any unwise haste we build upon the foundation, wood, hay, and stubble; or, lest by a suspicious caution, we reject gold, silver, and precious stones.

But while we agree to give up all uncommanded practices to fair examination, and to let them stand or fall by their respective merits, the case is totally different with regard to institutions which the Lord has appointed. He came as King of his Church: he gave laws which demand our obedience. We are not authorized to set these aside, that we may regulate the church by the taste of the times: the question is not, what are *our* terms, but what are the terms required by the Lord.

Here the Baptist takes high ground. He asks for no

more than was required in the Apostolic church. In the first instance, he asks for a declaration of faith in Christ. This, it is granted, he has a right to expect from every one who solicits communion. But if he and his brethren have pressed their inquiries on this subject with needless or distressing minuteness, and thus have hindered, rather than helped those who were desirous of walking in the ways of the Lord; he ought, whenever the point is proved, to acknowledge that he was in an error. He has no right to ask for more than a credible New-Testament profession. In the next place, he adds, the New Testament requires that believers should be baptised. In this sentiment, he is supported by nearly the whole christian community. That small part excepted, who deny the perpetuity of baptism, there is not one to be found, who will venture to assert, that the believer has discharged his duty to his Lord, if he is not baptised. On this ground then, we take our stand. According to the New Testament, a profession of faith and baptism on that profession, took place *previous* to a person's being considered as a Member of the church. In following such authority we are *not* raising a wall of separation which Christ has not raised; we are *not* requiring terms of our own devising; we are doing nothing more than what we find in the divine word. We maintain that we have no authority to call in question the appointments of our divine legislator, and since He *requires* believers to be baptised, on their becoming the visible subjects of his Kingdom, unless it be proved that baptism was temporary in its duration, we are bound to act upon the same plan. For as Dr. CAMPBELL justly observes, "when once a fence is established by statute, it is necessary, in order to support its authority, that the letter of the statute should be the rule in all cases" *.

We are aware it will be said, that this plan of receiving

* *Preliminary Dissertations to his translation of the Gospels.* Diss. vi. p. 4. § 11.

Members into the Church, keeps some at a distance who deserve to be esteemed, and does not always prevent improper characters from entering. But if this objection has any force, it proves that Jesus Christ was the author of an imperfect system, and that time has discovered its defects. Our object, however, is not to defend the wisdom of his appointments: though it might easily be shown, that his plans are more likely to be correct than ours, and that wherever men have departed from them, evils in abundance have poured themselves into the christian church.

Here, our Pædobaptist brethren will probably object, that we are assuming, at least a part of the question under consideration; that we are not contending for an Institution of Christ, but for that Institution as we practice it; that they think, neither the age of the subjects, nor the mode of administration essential to the ordinance; and that therefore the question concerning baptism in *our view*, and in *their view*, practically involves very different consequences.

We reply, we admit that the questions are different—whether we ought to receive those who allow that baptism is an Institution of Christ, and who plead that they have obeyed the command, though we think they have not;—and—whether we ought to receive those who either oppose or neglect the institution altogether. Nor do we blend these questions; they admit of a separate investigation, and are to be met by arguments entirely distinct. But in the controversy now before us, the query is not, whether Pædobaptism is a valid administration of the ordinance, for it is distinctly stated by Mr. Hall that Infant baptism is A NULLITY *(Reply, p. 5)*: and therefore the present discussion unavoidably leads to the inquiry, ought we to give up *Baptism* as no longer necessary to communion with the Christian Church; or, ought we to maintain it in its original situation? an inquiry which, though at first sight it seems to concern *us* only, yet in the issue, will involve principles, in which all who acknowledge the permanency of the ordinances of the gospel are deeply interested.

Since Mr. Hall began the present controversy, Dr. Mason of New York has published a second edition of a work entitled " A Plea for Catholic Communion in the Church of God." The first Edition was printed in America under the title of " A Plea for Sacramental Communion on Catholic Principles." The second was printed in London, while the author was visiting this country. Mr. Hall hails him as a brother, quotes his work with high approbation, tells us that Dr. M. acknowledged the justness of his leading principle, and is lavish in the praise of his new ally, at the expence of those Baptists who do not adopt the system of mixed communion. Yet whoever reads the Doctor's work with attention, will perceive that neither his reasonings nor his authorities, touch the present question. He has written a large volume to prove, that, "portions of two denominations" did right in "coming together on the broad ground of *one body, one spirit, one hope, one Lord, one faith, one baptism, one God and Father of all.*" Introd. p. xiii. His work proceeds on the supposition that the parties whom he designs to conciliate, are members of Churches, which have "the rightful possession of the Sacraments;" (p. 9, 10.) which, he observes, "is essential to the existence of a true church." These, he informs us, are two, Baptism and the Lord's Supper; he quotes the definition of the "Sacraments" given in the Wesminster Confession of Faith; and his whole argument supposes that both these "Sacraments" are viewed by each party in the same light, and practically regarded for the same ends. In the progress of his work he brings forth a long list of authorities to prove, that good men of various ages, have pleaded the cause of Christian union, and have zealously urged their brethren *who practised the same institutions in their respective Churches*, and who agreed in the belief of the same general system of doctrine, to commune together! These authorities were well adapted to Dr. Mason's purpose in justifying *his* uniting with Dr. Romeyn at New York; because the Churches under the pastoral care of these two ministers, were on the same general ground both respecting doctrine and practice; but how they would have applied, if one of these Churches had been in the opinion of the other *unbaptised*, Dr. Mason does not inform us. Every person at all acquainted with Ecclesiastical History knows, that communion in the Lord's supper always supposed the previous baptism of the parties; and that the authorities, so abundantly quoted in the Doctor's " Plea," are perfectly nugatory, when applied to the case of those who believe that the parties to whom they object are *not baptised*.

Dr. Mason thinks he has furnished " a sure and easy rule of conscience in regard to church fellowship, viz. no particular act of communion is to be interpreted as reaching beyond *itself*, unless coupled with other acts by an *express* or *known* condition." (p. 329.) We have no objection to apply this " sure and easy rule" to the case which concerns our present enquiry. The "*express*" or "*known* condition" which is " coupled " with every " act of communion" between Baptists and Pædobaptists must necessarily be " interpreted" as a declaration—either that the Baptist acknowledges Pædobaptism to be valid ; or, that he does not regard baptism to be at all requisite to Communion. The first, no Baptist can acknowledge ; the second, is the subject of the present inquiry, and, in our view, is attended with unanswerable objections: but neither of them concerns Dr. Mason's great object, which is to the last, to recommend communion among "those who profess ' one Lord, one faith, one baptism, one hope of their calling'." (*p*. 395.)

Notwithstanding this constant reference to a state of

opinions perfectly distinct from that before us in this controversy, Dr. Mason in the preface to his second edition, alludes to the present debate, and thinks proper to say, " that all such differences, *be they what they may,* are insufficient to justify the want of communion between those that mutually own and honor each other's christianity." (p. viii,) How he can reconcile this system with the sentiments of his own church does not appear. If the *Associate Reformed Church,* of which he is a member, acknowledge his theory in all its extent, they have far departed from the opinions of their forefathers; and if they do not see a difference between the communion of persons who use the same rites of baptism and the same formularies in other things, and the admission of those to communion who are without baptism, they have lost their former acuteness.

From Dr. Mason's work Mr. Hall anticipates very important results. " Let us hope that America, that land of freedom, where our pious ancestors found an asylum from the oppression of intolerance, will exert under the auspices of such men as Dr. Mason, a powerful reaction on the parent state, and aid her emancipation from the relics of *that pestilential evil,* still cherished and retained in too many British Churches." (*Preface, p.* viii, ix.)

What the American Baptists will do in future, time alone can discover. In times past, we are told that many of their churches acted on the plan of mixed communion; but they found that it so often both destroyed their peace and impeded their prosperity, that in a great variety of instances they have adopted the practise of communing with baptised believers only. BENEDICT, in his General History of the Baptist Denomination in America, printed in 1813, mentions a number of cases of this kind, and some churches, he says, have been "*split to pieces by the embarrassing policy.*" It is commonly supposed here in England, by the friends of that system, that if it was once admitted it would retain its influence; but whoever reads *Benedict's History*, will see that American experience does not favour such an expectation.

Mr. Hall observes, that "some whose character commands the deepest respect, are known to deprecate the agitation of the present controversy from an apprehension of the injury the denomination may sustain by the exposure of its intestine divisions." (*Preface p.* xiii.) Probably by this time they are satisfied that their apprehensions were well founded; so far, at least, as relates to the present effect of the discussion; for it cannot be imagined that they were afraid lest the cause of *truth*, on whichever side it was found, would ultimately be injured.

The opponents of our denomination seem to think that they have gained an advantage they never had before; they consider Mr. Hall's work as sacrificing one important part of our common system; and as making a concession which reduces the practical importance of baptism to nothing. With their views of baptism, the case of the unbaptised soliciting communion with them will be of such rare occurrence, that it will very seldom require consideration; but if Mr. Hall's sentiment prevails, they clearly see, that whenever a Pædobaptist wishes to unite with us, we shall be expected practically to declare, that the baptism for which we plead, however conformable to the primitive institution, has lost its authority, and is no longer to be retained in its original station. Hence the result is, that all who dislike the Baptists, and all who are inimical to the institution of baptism itself, with Mr. Hall at their head, are loud in their exclamations against us; and if they go as far as he does, in the extent and severity of their accusations, they can at least plead the sanction of *his* example in their defence. His writings clearly shew that he is in avowed friendship with those who oppose his own denomination; and that, according to his own statement, the points in which he differs from them are trifling, compared with those in which they are both agreed. Is it surprising that men of discernment, "whose character commands the deepest respect", and who knew the extent of Mr. Hall's theory, should have deprecated a system of which they saw this would be the effect? Perhaps they were also afraid lest it should separate the Baptists and Pædobaptists to a greater distance than before, or render their intercourse less confidential. But—the die is cast, and whatever consequences may follow, those who according to the New Testament believe that baptism should precede communion, have not to bear the blame of exciting this controversy; and they had no other option, but either to defend their cause; or—to sit down in silence, and bear the stigma of having nothing to say, or of not daring to speak: they have made their election, and leave the result to God.

They were compelled to defend themselves for the additional reason, that they viewed the opinion which Mr. Hall advocates, as in the end attacking the permanency of Baptism; and since he attempts to establish his theory as the law of the New Testament, it leads us directly to the question,—has the sacred volume nullified its own institutions, or does it still continue to support them?

With respect to the effect which the discussion has produced on the dispositions of the Baptists and Pædobaptists towards each other, as far as my observation has extended, the strict Baptists stand where they did; their conduct is not altered towards the members of other denominations, and I hope their temper is not injured; they are still willing to unite with their fellow christians on common ground in promoting a common cause; and I doubt not many of the Pædobaptists will go as far with us as they did before, and with the same general feeling. Some of them are aware that Mr. Hall's favorite theory relieves neither party from any difficulty. Others hold different language; and in proportion as they adopt his opinion, they occupy a new station. How far they will be affected by the change, time alone will discover.

Mr. Hall thinks that a "simple expedient" might settle the difficulty which arises from the divided opinion of a church, where the majority are in favor of mixed communion; which is, to "admit pious Pædobaptists, without hesitation, and to let those whose principles deter them from joining in such communion receive the Lord's supper apart." (*Preface p.* xviii.) The success of this plan is more than doubtful. What is to be done where the minister is of a different opinion from the majority? If such a system as this should become popular, every minister, of the sentiments now described, whatever may have been the length or importance of his services, would feel his confidence in those with whom he had long acted in unity, so sensibly weakened, that he would not be surprised at the rising of a storm that would drive him away. But besides the effect which this expedient might have on the minister, it would also produce an effect on the members whose sentiments did not agree with those of the majority. The *older members* especially, who had been labouring for a course of years in a common cause, would feel themselves deeply affected by such an alteration. What would they think, when they saw the constitution of that church subverted, the prosperity of which had been intimately connected with their purest enjoyments, and their most vigorous exertions? How admirably would this "expedient" promote the *unity* of the church, when those who maintain its original principles would in reality be expelled, instead of continuing to be recognised as joined to the Church in one body? What would they think of a scheme which under the pretence of increasing the members of Baptist Churches, admitted *Pædobaptists,* and *dissevered* BAPTISTS! Notwithstanding Mr. Hall says this can be done "without inflicting the slightest wound on these amiable and exemplary persons," (p. xviii) it would be found an impossibility. Many would never submit to the experiment; and of those that did, several would be found who would not repeat it. They would too strongly recollect past days, and too powerfully feel the alteration forced upon them, not to be filled with reflections which they would not wish to have excited again. Though Mr. Hall attempts to put his plan into smooth language, and if ever he means to conciliate, one would suppose it would be, when he was professing to treat those members of our Churches who differ from him with marked respect, as *"amiable and exemplary characters,"* yet there is a manner in which he speaks of them, which *ought not* and *cannot* escape their notice. " By this *simple expedient,"* we are told, " the *views of all parties* will be met : the *majority* will *exert* their *prerogative,* and *act consistently with their avowed principles:* the PÆDOBAPTISTS *will obtain their* RIGHTS ; and the *abettors of strict communion will enjoy that state of separation and seclusion which they covet!"* (p. xviii, xix.) Such expressions need no comment, and such doctrines require no elucidation. We are told, that *Pædobaptists* have a *right* to membership in *Baptist Churches*; the "*majority*" are instructed in defence of their "*prerogative*" and "*principle*" to admit that right; and the "abettors of strict communion" are held up to view, as if they *coveted* " *separation and seclusion,"* and would " *enjoy*" it, even though the churches of which they had been members were rending in pieces ! "By this means" says Mr. Hall "a *silent revolution* may be effected in our Churches :"—perhaps so ; silence is often produced by astonishment: one consequence would certainly follow, which at first takes place in silence; and that is, a want of confidence in those who were known to be the projectors or abettors of such a revolution. But in time, those who had been silent would speak, and it requires no sagacity to foresee what they would say.

But what would be the *effect* of this revolution ? To

exclude more members than would be added by the means of it. Generally speaking, the number of Pædobaptists who are found in Baptist Churches is small. When a Member of a Church holding mixed communion is asked, what is the state of the society to which he belongs, the answer is frequently in the tone of Apology;—" we are on the plan of open communion, but we have *very few* in our church except those who have been baptised." Thus they endeavour to justify themselves, and to persuade their brethren, that they may, with security, admit those Pædobaptists who wish to unite with them (whom it would be a pity to lose) because they are *so few,* that they cannot possibly do any hurt. Mr. Robinson says, "probably mixed fellowship and great majorities of unbaptised believers tending to alter the constitution of the church, may have been associated ideas. But whatever may have happened in some few particular cases, the connection is not good; for in most mixed churches where the minister is a baptist, *the proportion is not so great as five to a hundred*[*]."

Our denomination is supposed to lie under the "frown of the great head of the Church," as the consequence of *strict communion.* (*Preface, p.* xxiii, xxiv.) If so, it may reasonably be expected, that those churches which are upon the plan of open communion, are eminently blest with the divine presence, and that their success can be visibly traced to this cause.—It may be expected, that in proportion to the congregations, the churches are larger, that the conversion of sinners is more frequent, and that the amount of the real piety of the church and congregation is greater than in other places. In these congregations it may be expected, that the "advantage of overwhelming evidence in favour of our sentiments" (*Preface, p.* xxiii), is felt in all its power, and that there is a striking contrast between the blighted and withered state of a congregation

[*] *Doct. of Toleration in Miscel. Works, vol.* III. *p.* 188.

and church where strict communion is maintained, and the fruitful condition of that church in which open communion draws down the divine blessing. Mr. Hall has thrown out an insinuation, but has brought nothing to justify it. What he *has* said stands as an accusation against the body, and his authority, as one of the denomination, may be quoted in its support; while it is evident, that the defence is both delicate and difficult. In a former treatise we stated an opinion on the fact: and though that opinion is not altered, but confirmed, yet we would rather bear our own share of any man's censure, than excite the unpleasant and painful feelings, which would unavoidably be the effect of such a detail of facts and reasonings, as the defence of this part of our common cause would necessarily require; and we are sure many of our brethren would do the same.

But since it is commonly found, that the introduction of mixed communion sets baptism aside, as of very little moment, if our supposed want of success arises from our not adopting that system, the inference is neither distant nor unfair, that if we ceased to be Baptists we should be more useful still!

It seldom happens that a controverted subject continues long stationary. In the progress of the discussion, the ground will more or less be changed, and the subject viewed in its different bearings. When JOHN BUNYAN pleaded for mixed communion, he said, the rule by which he would receive persons into fellowship, was "by a discovery of their faith and holiness, and their declaration of their willingness to subject themselves to the laws and government of Christ in his Church." But he thought baptism of so little consequence, that when urged with the priority of baptism to communion, as recorded in the New Testament, he replied, "that water baptism hath formerly gone first is granted: but that it ought of necessity to do so, I never saw proof." In consistency with this theory, he pleaded for the reception of those who in his opinion were pious characters; and if they said, they did not see it their duty to be baptised, he was ready not only to accept of their apology, but to come forward in their defence. Alluding to the Israelites in the time of Joshua, who had not been circumcised in the wilderness, he says, " they could not have a bigger reason than this, ' I have no light therein,' which is the cause at this day that many a faithful man denieth to take up the ordinance of baptism. But I say whatever the hindrance was it mattereth not; our brethren have a manifest one, an invincible one, one that all the men on earth, nor angels in heaven cannot remove; for it is God that created light, and for them to do it without light, would but prove them unfaithful to themselves, and make them sinners before God*." The question however, is not, whether a person ought to act hypocritically; but, whether we are compelled by the word of God to receive those as members, who in our estimation, do not fulfil its directions, and give this as a reason, " we have no light therein."

BUNYAN also says, "the person that is to be baptised stands by that, a member of no church at all, neither of the visible, nor yet of the invisible. A visible saint he is, but not made so by baptism; for he must be a visible saint before, else he ought not to be baptised. Baptism makes thee no member of the church, neither particular nor universal; neither doth it make thee a visible saint; it therefore gives thee neither right to, nor being of, membership at all †:" Baptism is—" none of those laws, nor any part of them, that the church as a church should shew her obedience by;—I find not that baptism is a sign to any *but to the person that is baptised* ‡:" "If water baptism, as the circumstances with which the churches were pestered of old, trouble their peace, wound the consciences

---

*Bunyan's Confession of faith, and reasons of his practice, &c. Works, vol. I. p. 128, 135, 136, 8vo. Ed. 1769.   † *ibid.* p. 130.   ‡ p. 155, 156.

of the godly, dismember and break their fellowships, it is, *although an ordinance,* for the present, *to be prudently shunned:* for the edification of the church, as I shall shew anon, is to be preferred before it ‡."

Dr. JAMES FOSTER, who pleaded the same cause in a sermon on " Catholic Communion," raised the controversy afresh, and used arguments similar to those of Mr. Hall; but though Dr. Foster's popularity and talents were of a distinguished order, yet his system made no lasting impression on the public mind.

After that time mixed communion seems to have been commonly defended on the ground, that a person who believes himself to have been baptised, ought to be admitted to the Lord's Supper by those who may not think his views of baptism correct either with respect to the mode or subject. In opposition to arguments built on this basis, MR. BOOTH wrote his *"Apology for the Baptists:"* in which he pressed his opponents with the consequence, that in consistency with their method of reasoning, they ought to receive those who were *acknowledged* to be *unbaptised:* an inference which at that time very few were bold enough to admit.

When MR. ROBINSON appeared in the field, he constructed his argument on a ground considerably different from that of any of his predecessors; and Mr. Hall distinctly states that his work " rests on principles more lax and latitudinarian than it is in his power conscientiously to adopt." *(Terms of Communion, Pref. p.* ix.*)*

But he takes the consequence which Mr. Booth pressed on those who contended for mixed communion in his day; he admits that we may receive those who are unbaptised, knowing them to be such; and that although baptism is an institution still in force, yet baptism and communion have no connection whatever.

This theory places the inquiry on a basis, which, though

‡ *ut supra, p.* 136.

not altogether new, yet, we believe, was never so boldly and distinctly brought forward as at present. The subject which we have now to examine lies essentially in this single question; if we make the New Testament our rule, ought the church to be composed of persons who are *unbaptised?* If the rule *once* given to the Church, *once* universally obeyed, and acknowledged to be *still* in force, may be passed over, Mr. Hall's theory may be admitted. But then, the consequence will necessarily be, that the New Testament as the rule of our conduct in the church, will immediately become a useless book. For what possible authority can we attach to its directions, if we can set aside one of its plain and universal commands? In vain shall we plead its sanction in favour of any thing contrary to the spirit and taste of the times, when it may be replied, that according to the New Testament, church members should be baptised, but it is now acknowledged that such antiquated practices are not suitable to modern days. On this plan we have no ground of reasoning left, except that of mere *expedience.*

The whole spirit of the argument against us, strikes at the root of every thing by which both *dissenting* and *protestant* churches are distinguished. Charges of assumption, of infallibility, and of intolerance, are plentifully heaped upon us. These we consider not at all formidable. Had our forefathers been awed by such accusations, their posterity might still have been wearing the chains of superstition. The dominion of truth and evidence disdain such attempts to confine their sway. We assume nothing but the right of doing what we find commanded in the New Testament. If we mistake the sense of the sacred volume, we regret our misfortune: but the *principle,* that we ought to follow that infallible rule as our guide, we can never give up. For this principle we plead: that we should be reviled for maintaining it is nothing new; but we defy the ingenuity of any one to shew, how christians of any description can form a church according to the New Testament, without being liable to similar charges, from those who may choose to attack them.

When we urge the directions and precedents of the New Testament in favour of our practice, we are sometimes met by the reply, 'doubtless you think the inference correct, but others think differently': and the result is, 'you ought not to adopt a plan which is contrary to the conclusions drawn by other people'. A reply which would serve a Roman Catholic in opposition to every Protestant argument against Popish authority.

The question of the tendency of any opinion must in the end become a question of experience: but in the present instance, there are manifest consequences which we ought to anticipate. Many think (we doubt not sincerely) that mixed communion would promote our common cause. They imagine that it would bring a numerous accession of Pædobaptists into our congregations and churches: and this expectation increases the earnestness with which they plead for it. Lest, however, we should suppose, that their earnestness for the admission of persons unbaptised arises from indifference to the institution of baptism, they assure us, *that indeed they are Baptists,* and are not indifferent to what they think is the command of the Lord. During the period of discussion, their zeal in its favour may be preserved alive by various causes; but let the controversy pass away; let it be generally admitted, that baptism is not now a term of communion; that it is a duty which calls a person's attention only as an individual, but at present has no connection either with the right or privilege of being a member of a church; and that there is as ready an access to communion without it, as with it; and what must be the result? It will soon be considered a very unfortunate thing to have any discussion excited about an external rite. Those who are so deeply impressed with the propriety of believers' baptism, that they cannot be satisfied without it, will be advised to follow the dictates of their consciences, that they may obtain peace of mind. But though the Baptists will doubtless be gratified by such occurrences, yet if they embrace with ardour the system of mixed communion, they will be so neutralized by its influence, that they will be afraid of hearing their peculiar sentiment defended, lest any thing should be said that might hurt the minds of those who are *not* Baptists. Such a state of things may continue for a time, but it cannot be permanent. Either, one of the institutions of the Lord will disappear from the church; or the debate respecting it will be revived. Churches composed of persons whose sentiments widely differ, never continue long in peace, except one of the parties is so decided a minority as to be kept entirely in the back ground. When the English Baptists began to explain and defend their sentiments, they found it necessary to act by themselves, both for the enjoyment of peace, and the promotion of a common cause: and the consequences of the present discussion will be unlike those that have gone before, if our brethren are not ultimately convinced, that, unless they are disposed to sacrifice their principles, they must continue to bear reproach and persevere.

CHAPTER II.

ON THE STATEMENT OF THE CONTROVERSY.

Mr. Hall acknowledges that the point in debate between the advocates of open communion, and those who oppose it, is fairly stated in the work entitled "Baptism a Term of Communion," and that "*the question* and the *only question* is, whether those who are *acknowledged to be unbaptised ought to come to the Lord's Table.*" *(Reply p.* 1.*)* To this explicit concession we particularly request the reader's attention.

The inquiry next in order ought to be, by what rule *the question*, and the *only question* now in debate is to be determined. If by the New Testament, we then ask, does that volume sanction the admission of the unbaptised to communion? If it *does*, all that we can reasonably require is, *evidence* that we ought to admit them, and the controversy will be finished. If it does *not*, we are sufficiently justified in maintaining that Baptism *is* a term of communion; for no one who has read the New Testament will pretend to deny that the members of the Primitive Churches were baptised; and that baptism was esteemed essential to communion in the apostolic age. If we are referred to any other authority than the New

Testament, or to any reasons for admitting "those who are *acknowledged to be unbaptised*" which are not to be found there, we shall take our leave of the controversy. Our object is not to follow the wisdom of man, but the directions of the word of God. To use the words of Dr. Campbell we shall " desist from expatiating further on the absurdity of making that a doctrine of the Gospel, with which the New Testament does not acquaint us; or a christian institution, which did not commence till after the decease of the last of the Apostles." *

But though Mr. Hall grants that the question in debate is correctly stated, he finds great fault with the general view which is given of the controversy in the work now mentioned. The outline which is there sketched, scarcely needs either explanation or defence. The parties in the controversy, it was observed, are *Pædobaptists* on the one side, and *Baptists* on the other. The general sentiments of the Pædobaptists on the subjects of Baptism and Communion are first noticed; and then, the general sentiments of the Baptists as a body, on the same points :—and the controversy that arose between the two parties, both with respect to baptism and communion. Here it was stated, that the Baptists are divided into two classes : some oppose the admission of Pædobaptists to communion, because they consider them to be unbaptised, and believe, that admitting the unbaptised is not according to the direction of Christ, and the practice of his Apostles : others are willing to admit them, and plead for their admission by various arguments.

By this statement Mr. Hall is much offended; and though it is not desirable to protract the discussion, by following him step by step, there are a few things which ought not to be passed over in silence.

He objects, in the first place, to the account which is given of the sentiments of the Baptists. It was

* *Lect. on Ecc. Hist. Vol* 1. *p.* 103.

observed, that in their view, the subjects of baptism should be believers, that the ordinance should be administered by immersion; "and then, and not before, they consider such persons properly qualified, according to the New Testament, for the reception of the Lord's Supper." *(Baptism a Term of Com. p.* 11, *first Ed.)* But, we are told, " the last position Mr. K. is aware is not maintained by the Baptists as such, but by a part of them only: it may be doubted whether it be the sentiment of the majority. &c." *(Reply p.* 2.) In the second edition, this "position" was altered in the following manner; " and *as a body,* they believe that such persons are not till then, fully qualified according to the New Testament, for the reception of the Lord's supper." (*2d. Ed. p.* 11.) But this alteration would not remove Mr. Hall's objection, since the passage still continued to state, that the mixed communion Baptists are a minority of the denomination.

It was not suspected that on this point there was any difference of opinion, since Mr. Hall had fully acknowledged all that we stated. In his treatise on Terms of Communion, after he has described the sentiments of the Baptists, he adds, " On this ground they have for the MOST PART confined their communion to persons of their *own persuasion,* in which, illiberal as it may appear, *they are supported by the* GENERAL PRACTICE *of the Christian World*", &c. *(p.* 11.) "The advocates of strict communion are the *most numerous*; it is the GENERAL PRACTICE of our Churches." *(p.* 12.) Agreeably to this statement, he afterwards speaks of strict communion as the sentiment of "the MAJORITY of the Baptists"; and adds that he has 'presumed to resist the *current of opinion.*' *(p.* 87.) In the preface to his Reply, the same thing is clearly confessed. "From the appearance of Mr. Bunyan's treatise, entitled *Water Baptism no bar to Communion,* to the publication of the celebrated Mr. Robinson, a whole century elapsed, with few or no efforts to check the progress of the *prevailing system,* which had gained so firm a footing previous to Mr. Booth's writing, that he felt *no scruple* in entitling his defence of that practice, *An Apology for the Baptists.* The MAJORITY appear to have carried it with so high a hand, that the FEW CHURCHES who ventured to depart from the *established usage* were very equivocally acknowledged to belong to the general body, and seem to have been content to purchase peace, at the price of silence and submission." (*Preface p.* 11, 12.)

Thus we see, that when Mr. Hall wrote his *Terms of Communion,* and also when he wrote the Preface of his Reply to " *Baptism a Term of Communion*", the strict Baptists were acknowledged to be the MAJORITY. But when he was writing the second page of his Reply, his tone is changed, and, the " position" already noticed, he says, " Mr. K. is aware, is not maintained by the Baptists as such, but by a part of them only ; *it may be doubted whether it be the sentiment of* THE MAJORITY"!

Let the reader keep in view the reason given by Mr. Hall why " Mr. Booth felt no scruple in entitling his defence of that practice [strict communion] *An Apology for the Baptists*", which was, the " firm footing" obtained by the *prevailing* system ; and compare it with the following passage : "it is but just however to remark, that this disposition to *enlarge* the number of his partizans, is not peculiar to this writer. Mr. Booth when engaged in defending a thesis, about which the Baptists had long been divided, chose *in the same spirit* to denominate his performance *An Apology for the Baptists.*" (*Reply p.* 2.) How these differences are to be reconciled I know not.

Mr. Hall adds, "Our author proceeds to observe, 'Here arises a controversy between the two parties, not only respecting baptism, but also respecting their conduct to each other on the subject of communion.' Where, let me ask, are the traces to be found of this *imaginary* controversy between the Baptists and Pædobaptists on that subject?" (*Reply p.* 3.) We answer, wherever the question has been agitated; wherever Pædobaptists have sought admittance among Baptists; wherever their friends have attempted to introduce them into churches which had not been in the practice of mixed communion. Such circumstances have frequently taken place, and they have seldom failed to produce some degree of discussion.

Mr. Hall asks, "what are the names of the parties, and to what publications did it give birth?" *p.* 3. That the Pædobaptists are "parties" in opposition to our views of Communion he himself acknowledges afterwards; he says, he has "no doubt the result of an accurate and extensive enquiry" into their sentiments would be in favour of his opinion. p. 10. As to the publications to which it gave birth, we need mention only BOOTH'S *Apology for the Baptists*. That one work fully proves all that we have stated. In the Preface, Mr. Booth says, " it is entirely on the DEFENSIVE that the Author takes up his pen; for had not the principles and practice of those professors who are invidiously called *Strict Baptists*, been severely censured by MANY THAT MAINTAIN, and by *some* who deny the divine authority of Infant Baptism, these pages would never have seen the light."

Mr. Hall continues his attack: " this author had informed us at the distance of a few lines, that the Pædobaptists in general believe that none ought to come to the Lord's table who are not baptised. *If this is correct*, we may indeed easily conceive of their being offended with us for deeming them unbaptised; but how our refusal to admit them to communion should become the subject of debate, is utterly mysterious." (*p.* 3.)

" *If this is correct*"— Does Mr. Hall mean to say that it is not correct? If it is *not*, Mr. Hall was either *incorrect* when he wrote " on Terms of Communion", or a change in the sentiments of the Pædobaptists has taken place since he published that work. There he distinctly stated, that the Baptists " have for the *most part* confined their communion to persons of their own persuasion, in which, illiberal as it may appear, *they are supported by the general practice of the christian world,* which, whatever diversities of opinion may have prevailed, have *pretty generally concurred in insisting upon baptism as an* INDISPENSIBLE PREREQUISITE to the Lord's table." (*Terms of Com. p.* 11.) Again, he confesses that the conduct of the baptists arises " from a rigid adherence to a principle almost *universally* adopted, that baptism is, under all circumstances, a necessary prerequisite to the Lord's Supper." (*p.* 12.)

But, says Mr. Hall in the latter part of his sentence, "how our refusal to admit them [the Pædobaptists] to communion should become the subject of debate is utterly mysterious." The mystery is easily explained; the Pædobaptists have taken two grounds of argument; in general they have agreed with us, that baptism should precede communion, but they say, this ought not to be pressed so far, as to make a profession of faith, and immersion, essential to the ordinance. They do not say, baptism cannot be administered by immersion; but they maintain, that immersion is not necessary to its administration. Hence they complain of us, because we cannot admit that the sprinkling of Infants is Christian baptism. This is the ground of many of the charges of bigotry and intolerance, which are preferred against us; the amount of which is; if we would give up our sentiments and and allow their practice to be baptism, the two parties might unite very well: but because we cannot go this length, they instantly see the consequence, that on their own principles, a separation of communion is unavoidable. Others have adopted the wider theory of our author; that joining in communion neither supposes a person to have been baptised nor the contrary: and Mr. Hall believes that this is the opinion of the majority of the Pædobaptists. If so, it has been adopted only a short time; for it is manifestly *not* the sentiment which they have been accustomed to profess; and it deserves their consideration, whether in admitting it, they do not as far depart from the principles of the New Testament, as from those of all the Pædobaptist Churches of the Reformation.

Mr. Hall thinks proper to add, " the truth is,— *nor could the writer be ignorant of it*,—that the dispute respecting communion existed in our own denomination, and in that only." (*Reply p.* 3, 4,) What Mr. Hall may call " the dispute," is not easy to determine; but I shall only observe in addition to the evidence already adduced, that no one acquainted with the history of Dissenters, since the year 1644, when the Baptists published their confession of faith, is ignorant that their opinions and practice, on the subject of communion, have at different times excited the attention of the Pædobaptists, and exposed them to a variety of censures.*

If Mr. Hall's principle is admitted, the christian world will undergo a complete *Revolution*; and the basis of nearly all the churches of which it is composed will be *overturned*. He seems to have completely seen this consequence when writing his introductory remarks to his first work. He there says, (*p.* 12.) " I am greatly mistaken if it be possible to bring it to a satisfactory issue, without adverting to topics in which *the christian world*

* *Vide*—JOHN GOODWIN'S Water dipping no firm footing for church communion, or considerations proving it not simply lawful, but necessary also in point of duty, for persons baptised in the *new* mode of dipping to continue communion with those churches, or embodied societies of saints of which they were members before the said dipping, &c. Lond. 1653. *And, a long answer to the question* " Whether it be our duty to seek peace with the Anabaptists," in BAXTERS Life and Times, by Sylvester, part 2, *p.* 181. *Also*, COTTON MATHER'S Ecclesiastical History of *New England*, (*book* vii. *ch.* 4.) for a view of the subject taken by the American divines: *and*, DR. MASON on Communion, *p.* 251.

are not less interested than the Baptists. If the conclusions we shall endeavour to establish appear on impartial inquiry to be well founded, it will follow that *serious errors* respecting terms of communion have prevailed to *a wide extent* in the Christian Church." In prosecuting this design, he begins by an attack upon us; we are to be the first sacrifice, but the above passage plainly shews that we are not to be the *last*. To say therefore, that the Pædobaptists " have no interest in the inquiry " (*p.* 9.) before us is absurd. The principle on which we plead for strict communion, they have asserted as a scriptural principle, times without number; and before it can be proved that they " have no interest in the inquiry, " they must unsay, what their confessions and elementary works on the subject of theology, have said in every variety of form; and a doctrine in complete opposition to what has been admitted with unprecedented universality, must be brought forward, as the happy discovery of modern times.

That the Pædobaptists and ourselves differ respecting both the mode and subjects of baptism, is nothing to the present purpose. They either *have*, or they have *not* founded their churches on the professed principle, that baptism ought to precede communion. Mr. Hall has confessed that this was " a principle almost *universally* adopted": how then can he affirm that they " have no interest in the inquiry", when one of the constitutional principles of their churches must be surrendered, if his theory is received?

In the Apostolic age, Mr. Hall confesses no such thing existed as an unbaptised Member of the Church. In the succeeding ages prior to the introduction of Popery, he acknowledges that the unbaptised were not admitted. At the Reformation, the principle acted upon in the purest ages was again recognised in all the Protestant churches: and the Non-conformists so generally declared their full acquiescence in it, that it would be difficult to find a single exception. If, then, the Pædobaptists "have no interest in the inquiry"; if, with Mr. Hall, they assert, that partaking of the Lord's Supper neither supposes a person to be baptised, nor the contrary; they will in direct terms oppose a principle on which their churches have generally been founded; and render further evidence of their being *parties* entirely unnecessary.

Undoubtedly it would be very agreable to Mr. Hall, and to those Pædobaptists who agree with him, if all this was forgotten. But that is impossible. It is deeply engraven in the records of time; and cannot be denied.

Should it be said that this relates to a point of *History*, that it does not decide the question of right, and that the Pædobaptists are now coming round to Mr. Hall's new system; we reply, if so, we admit that one of the aspects of the present controversy will be changed: but the consequence will be, that we shall soon arrive at the predicted result;—we shall have to contend not only for the *place* which baptism is to have in the christian Church, but for the *institution itself*.

Mr. Hall objects to our detail of the different reasons advanced in favour of mixed communion; and says, "of this diversity in the mode of defending our practice, the writer of these pages confesses himself *totally ignorant*." (*Reply p.* 4.) He goes so far as to say, "it is easy to perceive that the alledged disagreement in our principles is a *mere phantom.*" (*p.* 5.) We shall trouble the reader with only two remarks on these singular assertions.

First, Mr. Hall seems to have forgotten what he himself said in his "Terms of Communion." (*Pref. p.* ix.) He there assigns a reason why he does not notice the treatise of Mr. Robinson on mixed communion, which is, "because it rests on principles more lax and latitudinarian, than it is in his power conscientiously to adopt." By his own confession, he and Mr. Robinson "constructed defences" of their common sentiment on principles " totally dissimilar." In " Baptism a Term of Communion" it was stated, that the friends of mixed communion pleaded for their practice by various arguments; among others, "that as their Pædobaptist brethren think themselves baptised, they are willing to admit them on that ground, since they do not object to baptism itself, but only differ from others in the circumstantials of the ordinance." This is one of the two passages which Mr. Hall has quoted*, and the only one to which his charge of a diversity in the mode of defence can attach; for the remaining quotation contains his own theory on the subject.

In a letter intitled "A modest plea for free communion," said to be written by a venerable minister who died many years ago, is the following passage; " besides, it should be considered, who is to be the judge of what is, or is not Baptism in this dispute? Most certainly *every man for himself*, and not one for the other; else we destroy the right of private judgment, and go about to establish a Popish infallibility against the liberty of the Gospel. I have no business with any man's conscience but my own, unless by endeavouring better to instruct it, where it appears to be wrong. If my Pædobaptist brother *is satisfied in his mind, that he is rightly baptised, he is so to himself*, and while the answer of a good conscience attends it, God will, and *does own him in it*, to all the ends designed by it, so that while he considers it as laying him under the same obligations to holiness of heart and and life, as I consider my baptism to do me, why should not he commune with me at the table of our common Lord?" The date of this letter is June, 1772, and it is signed " PACIFICUS". In the year 1778 Mr. Booth published his " Apology for the Baptists;" in that work he frequently refers to this letter, and quotes part of the

---

* *A slight error excepted, which occurred probably in transcribing.*

above passage. See p. 59 of the first edition, p. 78, 79 of the edition printed in 1812. In his " Defence of Pædobaptism examined," in answer to Dr. Williams, printed in 1792, he again refers to the same passage. (See p. 50.) Subsequent to Mr. Booth's " Apology," Mr. Robinson stated the same mode of reasoning in his " Doctrine of Toleration," first printed in 1781. There we find the following passages; the first of which is quoted, chiefly for the purpose of enabling the reader to perceive the full bearing of the second. " We affirm that it is just, right, and agreable to the revealed will of Christ, that Baptist Churches should admit into their fellowship such persons as desire admission on profession of faith and repentance, although they refuse to be baptised by immersion, because they sincerely believe they have been baptised by sprinkling in their infancy." *Miscell. Works, Vol. III, p.* 154. Again, " we do not plead, then, for the admission of such a person, because we think he hath been baptised, for in our own opinion he hath not; but *because he judges he has been baptised*, and we have no authority to deprive him of the right of private judgement, but on the contrary, we are expressly commanded to allow him the liberty of determining for himself." (*p.* 168.) Mr. Hall has a right to inform us on what subjects he is " *totally ignorant* ;" and it is possible that he may not have had occasion to refer to all the above authorities; but it cannot be forgotten, not only that he expressly refers to Mr. Robinson's work, but that he distinctly professes " to answer" the treatise of " the late venerable Mr. Booth ;" yet from the writings of both these eminent men we learn, that the " mode of defending" mixed communion in their day, was very different from that adopted by Mr. Hall.

Mr. Fuller furnishes us with similar evidence, in his Letter on the subject of Communion. Speaking of the grounds of argument in favour of mixed communion, he says, "As far as I am *acquainted* with them, they may be reduced to two questions, which are these; 1—Has baptism any such instituted connexion with the Lord's Supper as to be a prerequisite to it? 2—*Supposing it has, yet if the candidate consider himself as having been baptised, ought not this to suffice for his being treated by a christian church as a baptised person;* and does not an error concerning the mode or subjects of Christian baptism come within the precept of the New Testament which enjoins forbearance, and allows every man to be fully persuaded in his own mind?" *Letter, p.* 9. The second of these questions, contains precisely the reason which we had stated. Mr. Fuller's extensive knowledge of the state of religious opinion few will deny; and he expressly tells us he was " acquainted" with an argument, of the existence of which Mr. Hall confesses his ignorance.

This is a sufficient refutation of his assertions, that, " whatever prejudices our cause may sustain, it has not been injured by that which results from intestine dissention": and—" it is easy to perceive that the alledged disagreement in our principles is a *mere phantom*."(*Reply p.* 4, 5.)

But, *Secondly*, even if I had not been able to refer to such clear evidence of a diversity in the defence of mixed communion from printed authorities, still the truth of what I have asserted would not have been affected. I have heard the arguments which I have mentioned in "Baptism a term of communion," urged against the practice which I have advocated. I have also heard other arguments, less honourable to the cause of mixed communion pleaded in its defence, but which in a cool investigation of the subject did not appear deserving of examination, and were passed over without notice: and therefore in the conscious integrity of not having alledged *phantoms*, but *facts*, my reply is brief.— " What I have written, I have written."

We shall close this chapter by a short sketch of a few

of the leading features of Mr. Hall's system. He confesses that baptism was, in the primitive church, universally required previous to communion, and that in the days of the apostles it was indispensible as a term of fellowship—but that *now* it is not necessary for that purpose; and he contends, that a church which acknowledges baptism to be one of the ordinances of the gospel, and an ordinance of perpetual obligation, not only may neglect to require obedience to it; but is justified in so doing by the directions of the New Testament.

His system is *not*, that we ought to receive those to communion *as* baptised, who believe themselves baptised, on the ground, that in their own estimation they have fulfilled this part of the will of Christ: for this argument he rejects, aware of its invalidity. But it is;—that we ought to receive the *unbaptised* knowing them to be so, provided we believe that they are conscientious in refusing to be baptised, and that we ought to admit them in obedience to the exhortations in the New Testament to receive those who are weak in the faith; though it is manifest that all such exhortations respect those who were *already* baptised, and who *had been* previously admitted into the Christian Church.

Again, Mr. Hall has thought proper to *assume*, that in order to prove the necessity of baptism prior to the reception of the Lord's Supper, "it is necessary to shew the dependance of one [institution] on the other; not merely that they are both clearly and unequivocally injoined; but that the one is prescribed *with a view* to the other." (*Reply p.* 13.) So that neither the authority by which they were enjoined, nor their perpetuity, nor the obligation to attend both, nor the order in which they are placed, nor the constant practice of the whole apostolic church, either separately or unitedly, justify us in requiring what the apostles required, if it cannot be proved, that either of the ordinances was prescribed *with a view* to the other.

Finally, Mr. Hall requires, that "some declaration of scripture be exhibited, which distinctly *prohibits* the celebration of the Lord's Supper by any person, who from a misconception of its nature, has omitted the baptismal ceremony." (*Reply p.* 14.) Thus we are called upon to admit the unbaptised to communion, because it is *not prohibited!* A mode of reasoning which might be applied to many other things with equal force.

Such is the system which our author has avowed: and such are the singular proofs that we are required to produce, in order to justify our conformity to the practice of the Apostles! We now proceed to other parts of our plan. In the mean time, we request the reader seriously to consider, as a general inquiry affecting the whole of the system which Mr. Hall advocates, how far the reception of those to communion who are *professedly unbaptised*, can agree with the eulogium which the Apostle Paul bestowed on the Corinthians, "Now I praise you, brethren, that ye remember me in all things, and *keep the ordinances*, AS *I delivered them unto you.*" 1 *Cor.* xi, 2.

CHAPTER III.

Mr. Hall's reasonings, in the second and third chapters of his reply, examined.

SECTION I.

Statement of the principle on which the present discussion depends,— Mr. Hall's arguments respecting our Lord's Commission examined.

The second and third chapters of Mr. Hall's work contain a long and laboured discussion, *professing* to examine the arguments alledged in " Baptism a term of Communion" in favour of the connection between the two positive institutions of the New Testament; but in reality passing them over.

For the purpose of keeping in view the true state of the controversy, it is necessary to remind the reader, that in the work to which Mr. Hall replied, the New Testament representations were brought forward as the ground of our argument;—the commission which the Lord gave to his disciples was first adduced as the *Law* of baptism;—the practice of the Apostles was exhibited as a *Commentary* on the Law;—the baptism of the primitive Christians, it was observed " was the term of professing their faith, by the special appointment of the Lord himself;" and after various observations on the subject, it was added, " From the whole, we derive one *obvious* PRINCIPLE, that baptism was intended to be a visible evidence of connection with the Christian Church." (*Baptism &c. p.* 17, 18, 21.) This is a brief outline of the first part of the argument, terminating in a proposition generally allowed, and which, if not proved to be a mistake, is of material consequence in the present discussion.

From the place assigned to baptism in the commission which the Lord gave to his Apostles, it *necessarily* preceded both Church membership, and Communion: and unless it can be proved, either, that it was not intended to be a visible evidence of a person's entering upon a Christian profession, and of his being united with the body of Christians;— or, that the design and place of the institution is altered by time, it ought to hold the same situation still. This is so evidently the impression made on the minds of serious thoughtful men, that it would be a difficult thing to find a single conscientious professor of the Gospel, who acknowledges the perpetuity of baptism, that would attempt to come to the Lord's table if he considered himself to be *unbaptised*.

The great point contended for in the second Chapter of " Baptism a term of Communion," is, that an examination of New Testament language, and New Testament facts, conducts us to the PRINCIPLE already mentioned. It is worthy of remark, that Mr. Hall does not take any notice of this principle: his object was a very different one: he employed himself in criticising some of the expressions used in that chapter, but the hinge on which the whole of that part of the discussion turned, he thought proper to overlook. But unless he can disprove this principle, he must defend his system on a ground on which he has not ventured to place it, or his cause is ruined. The principle, however, is so direct an inference from the

New Testament representations that it will bear every kind of fair investigation. Ingenuity may raise objections against it; false system and prejudice may obscure it; but it is so evidently the native dictate of the sacred volume, that it despises opposition ; and however it may be trampled upon, will in time regain the ascendancy.

On this point the strict Baptists and the great body of the Pædobaptists have been hitherto agreed ; and the mixed communion Baptists are left in a singular predicament, pleading for a right of access to the Lord's table on a ground, which no thoughtful man, who believes the perpetuity of baptism, dares venture to act upon *for himself*.

This single consideration suggests a general, but a powerful objection against Mr. Hall's reasoning. He says, receive the Pædobaptists, and receive them *as unbaptised*; but we ask, how can *they* come, and how can *we* receive them *in that Character?* Before this can be done, each party must agree to a plan, which both admit is contrary to the tenour of the New Testament.

To bring them to this point, Mr. Hall lays down a position, that the conditions of Communion and of salvation are the same; so that nothing is essential to communion, but what is essential to salvation. But before we admit this position, he must prove that we are not bound to follow the directions of the New Testament *as rules of conduct*, except in relation to duties which, in the strongest sense of the terms, *are essential to salvation*. Unless this can be demonstrated, Mr. Hall's argument is of no force ; for if the will of Christ ought to be our rule, it ought to be obeyed in the least as well as in the greatest of his commandments ; and that, not because we esteem both to be of equal importance, but because we are bound to obey whatever we clearly perceive to be his revealed will. So that the question which we have to settle is, not whether baptism is, or is not essential to salvation; but, whether according to the will of Christ it ought not to *precede* communion.

In many parts of Mr. Hall's work, he labours hard to represent us as unchristianising the Pædobaptists; so that if he cannot compel us to give up what we think is truth, he will at least, to the utmost of his power, exhibit us as objects of hatred. Every one who has read " Baptism a term of Communion," has had the opportunity of seeing, that the argument is there placed on a footing perfectly consistent with our maintaining a good opinion of those who differ from us. There is a wide difference between saying to the Pædobaptists, we think you wrong both respecting the mode and subjects of baptism and therefore we cannot unite with you; and saying,— your profession is so defective that it is incompatible with your Salvation. We *have* said,— " it would be criminal in either party to give up what they are convinced is the command of the Lord; but without judging each other, let us walk in that path which we each think most agreeable to the New Testament;" (*Baptism &c. p.* 40.) but we have *not* said, and we do *not* feel that we are at all compelled to say, that the Pædobaptists are cut off from the hope of Salvation, as the result of any of the principles which we have advocated.

The reader ought to be reminded, that it is in connection with one of those representations on which Mr. Hall makes some of his most severe animadversions, that it is said;—"here I am particularly desirous of not being misunderstood; it is *the principle* for which I *now* contend, and not its application to my own ideas." For, it is observed, if the Pædobaptists could prove infant baptism to be the will of Christ, and could convince the Baptists that they have been in the wrong, "still *the principle* will remain unimpeached, that baptism ought to hold the place it once held, as a *visible evidence of connection with the Christian Church.* (*p.* 21, 22.) In consistency with this sentiment, our endeavours were chiefly directed against Mr. Hall's position that the UNBAPTISED might be admitted to the Lord's Supper; and the argument was built upon ground held in common by us and the general body of the Pædobaptists. That the difference between us and them produces a separation of Communion we own; and we contend that it ought to do so, not because we think them in a fatal error, in consequence of their views of baptism, but because we conceive, that we are bound to adhere to what we believe is the primitive rule; not only by being ourselves baptised on a profession of faith, but also by maintaining in our churches the ordinances of the Lord, as they were first delivered. The expressions which Mr. Hall criticises we will examine; and hope we shall be able clearly to show that his interpretation is not the result of fair exposition; and that there is no connection between the reasonings of the strict Baptists, and the inferences which he draws from them.

The first thing in order, and the first that is noticed by Mr. Hall is the *Law of Baptism*, as it appears in the commission which the Lord delivered to the Apostles. Mr. Hall says, "we are as ready to allow as Mr. Kinghorn, that baptism was enjoined by the Apostolic commission; we are perfectly agreed with him respecting the *law* of baptism, and are accustomed to explain its nature, and inforce its authority, by the same arguments as he himself would employ." The mode, the subjects, and the perpetuity of the institution, he states in the manner that is done by baptists in general. "But," he says, "where the inquiry turns, not on the nature or obligation of baptism, but on the *necessary dependence* of another institution upon it, we are at a loss to perceive in what manner the quotation" [of the commission] "applies to the question before us. To us it is inconceivable how any thing more is deducible from the *law* of baptism, than its present and perpetual obligation. The existence of a law, establishes the obligation of a correspondent duty and nothing more." *Reply p.* 16, 17.

Here it is granted, that the *law* of baptism establishes a correspondent duty; that we may know what that duty is, let the law be considered. The first thing that will strike the mind of an inquirer is, that according to the appointment of Jesus Christ, baptism was to be administered to those who believed the Gospel: and that the Apostles were then directed to teach them *" to observe"* all things, whatsoever the Lord commanded them. If there be any meaning in words, baptism was the first ritual service which the believer was required to obey. Whatever Ordinances the Lord had commanded his disciples *"to observe"* besides, he himself places after baptism; and no ingenuity can reverse the order.

Previous to a person's submitting to baptism, he might, or he might not know the extent of that obedience which the Gospel required of its professors, according to the circumstances in which he had been placed; but when he had professed his faith in Christ, and had been baptised in his name, he then visibly subjected himself to his authority, and was bound to obey him in all those commands which followed the acknowledgement of him as his Lord.

Thus in the law itself we see the *priority* of baptism, both to a regular connection with the Christian Church, and to the Lord's Supper; it was prescribed in that order, and we have no choice; we must either give it that place, or practically declare that we do not act according to the direction of the primitive institution. One of the ordinances must necessarily precede the other, and no one will contend that on any interpretation, Communion was intended to come before baptism.

Mr. Hall has asserted that a participation of the Lord's supper neither implies that a person is baptised nor the contrary.* If the New Testament is taken as our guide, the baptism of those who are found at the Lord's supper *is* implied; for how could they come there to partake of an Institution in which a profession of his name is supposed, if they have not attended to that ordinance which, from its *nature*, as well as from the *order* of its appointment, necessarily preceded a visible, declared connexion with the Christian Church? He who denies the perpetuity of baptism, must be encountered with arguments which establish its continuance, but if its perpetuity as a christian ordinance is acknowledged, the inference is immediately seen, that he cannot consistently come to the Lord's table, unless he believes himself baptised. Persons who have not had their minds directed to the subject, or have been influenced by those, who thought baptism of no consequence, may have acted otherwise; but these are exceptions of a class against which no rule could make provision.

If the Apostolic Commission is of any importance as the rule of our conduct, it also follows that no church ought to receive an unbaptised person to communion. For, if the qualifications of candidates for Membership be examined by the directions given by the Lord himself, how can it be imagined, that submission to an institution which he commanded his disciples universally to obey, is not requisite. The Church depends for its existence on the Appointment of Christ, and the commission contains its constitutional principles. No class of persons whatever, has any authority to unite and act *as a Church*, except according to the rule which he has given; and therefore, any member is justified in objecting to the admission of "those who are acknowledged to be unbaptised," because it would be in manifest opposition to the direction of the head of the church.

* "It neither implies that they [the Pædobaptists] are baptised, nor the contrary; it has no retrospective view to that ordinance whatever."— *Terms of Com.* p. 97

The commission was designed to be a guide to the Apostles, as Ministers of Christ, and unless it be proved, that it is no guide to succeeding Ministers, it is their duty to examine it, and to follow its directions. Whatever difference of opinion has arisen concerning the mode and subjects of baptism, the *order* in which the ordinances of the Gospel are placed, is as intelligible as ever it was; but how are those guided by it who reverse its directions, and receive persons whom they plainly *acknowledge* are *unbaptised*? Whenever they cease to follow the prescribed order, they ought to shew that the authority of the commission has passed away, so that they have deviated from its directions, only because it no longer demands their attention.

In the progress of Mr. Hall's observations we meet with a singular deviation from the fair use of the term *law*, when he is criticising the expression before quoted, " the *law* of baptism." At the first, he seems to consider it as meaning, the direction and command which were contained in the commission; so far he is correct; this was the intended sense of the term. But before he has finished his page, we find him on different ground. He acknowledges that "Pædobaptists of all denominations have failed in a certain part of their duty"; "but" he adds, "if we are immediately to conclude from thence that they are disqualified for Christian Communion, we must seek a church which consists of members *who have failed in no branch of their obedience*; and must consequently despair of finding fit communicants apart from the Spirits of just men made perfect. Examine the idea of *law* with the utmost rigour, turn it on all sides, and it will present nothing beyond the obligation to a certain species of conduct, so that if Pædobaptists are really disqualified for the Lord's Supper, it must be for some other reason than their non-compliance with a *law*, or otherwise we must insist upon the refusal of every individual *who has not discharged all his obligations.*" Reply p. 17, 18.

In this quotation, (if I understand him) he argues as if the debate related to a question of obedience to the whole *moral law*, and as if perfect obedience was the required condition of membership. But according to that mode of reasoning we must not urge any thing that Christ has laid down as a rule of conduct in his Church; since in every instance it may be alledged against us, that for the same reason, " we must insist on the refusal of every individual who has not discharged *all his obligations*"! Thus we are left without a rule, for a law that we must not follow is of no practical use. Jesus Christ however, *did* give such a precept; and because he enjoined it, his Apostles *did* obey it. If then we "must insist" on perfection in the candidate for Communion, because we consider the Apostolic Commission *a law*; they doubtless did the same; for it is clear that they acted upon it as such, in submission to the authority, of their Lord. Let then Mr. Hall apply his objections to their conduct: we are content to take our share of blame in such company.

SECTION II.

Mr. Hall's arguments, respecting Apostolic Precedent, examined.

THE next subject of discussion is *Apostolic Precedent*, and a laboured attempt is made to weaken its force. It cannot be denied, that the Apostles and primitive Ministers *did* require baptism, previous to the Lord's Supper. Mr. Hall therefore thinks it necessary to account for their conduct in a manner that may sanction the admission of the *unbaptised* to communion *now*, and thus liberate us from all obligation to follow their example. In the style of apology we are told, "that" [as to baptism] "at that period no good men entertained a doubt respecting its nature,—that it was impossible they should, while it was exemplified before their eyes in the practice of the Apostles and Evangelists—that he who refused to abide by the decision of inspired men, would necessarily have forfeited his claim to be considered as a christian—that a new state of things has arisen, in which from a variety of causes, the doctrine of baptism has been involved in obscurity—that some of the best men put a different construction on the language of scripture from ourselves—and that it is great presumption to claim the same deference with the Apostles, and treat those who differ from us on the sense of scripture, as though they avowedly opposed themselves to Apostolic authority." (*Reply p.* 20.) From all which, it is designed that the reader should draw the inference, that we need not follow the Apostles as our guides, but may admit the *unbaptised*, although we are certain that they did not.

Again, it is asserted, that we " think differently of the

state of the unbaptised from what the Apostles thought;" *(p. 27)* and it is asked, whether we " form the same judgment of the present *Pædobaptists* as the apostles would have entertained of such as continued unbaptised in their day." (*p.* 26, 27.) Farther, that "to be unbaptised at present is, in a moral view, a very *distinct thing*, and involves very different consequences, from being in that predicament in the times of the Apostles."(*p.* 29.) Hence Mr. Hall would bring us to a confession, that his practice "is not opposed to Apostolic precedent, because that precedent respects a *different thing*." (*Reply, p*. 30.) Thus he attempts to cut off the whole at a stroke, by endeavouring to persuade us, that the conduct of the Apostles is after all, *not* a precedent for *us*; and although it shews how they understood and applied the command respecting baptism, yet *we* are not bound in submission to their authority, to walk in the same path, because we are not in the same circumstances. A short and effectual way of freeing ourselves from obligation to follow *their* example, in every thing, which does not suit our inclination.

All these statements are mere palliations of a line of conduct, undeniably opposed to that which was universal in Apostolic times. But let us attend to the expressions before quoted a little more particularly. "At that period" (in the Apostolic age) " no good men entertained a doubt respecting its nature," [viz. of baptism]—that it was impossible they should, while it was exemplified before their eyes in the practice of Apostles and Evangelists." This will be granted by all parties, but offers no reason why those who are satisfied that their views agree with the primitive church ought not to follow their convictions.—"That he who refused to abide by the decision of inspired men would necessarily have forfeited his claim to be considered as a Christian," is true; and he who should *at present* refuse to abide by their decision, no church would admit on any pretence whatever. But if the decision of the primitive ministers was of such consequence *then*, is their known and acknowledged conduct of no authority *now*? Was the conduct of the Apostles designed to be the guide of the Church, and intended to be held forth as an explanation of the will of Christ—or was it not? If it *was* we are bound to follow it, whenever we see by repeated examples, how they interpreted a general and perpetual rule of their Lord: and if on examination we are satisfied that they *did* require baptism prior to communion, we are in consistency bound to require the same. If we do not, we declare that inspired guides are of no use. If the conduct of the Apostles ought not to be our guide, let it be proved that we are mistaken in our opinion of its importance, that we may not have the trouble of examining that which is after all of no authority. On the plan for which Mr. Hall pleads, the rule of our conduct is gone, we are left to act on a system of *expediences*; and the New Testament rather exhibits the *Antiquities* of the Christian Church, than an example how the Apostles followed Christ and how we are to follow them.

But we are told, "that a *new state* of things has arisen, in which from a variety of causes, the doctrine of baptism has been involved in obscurity." In a certain sense this is true; it is a *new state* of things indeed which has arisen, when those who acknowledge the divine appointment and the permanency of baptism, argue that it is not necessary to Communion, and that Church fellowship, even where the perpetuity of baptism is believed, neither supposes that a person is baptised, nor the contrary. This was not the case in the primitive times, nor in any succeding period, till we arrive at discoveries of modern date. "Some of the best of men put a different construction on the language from ourselves:" suppose they do, are we bound to adopt their "construction" in opposition to the "overwhelming evidence in favour of our sentiments?"

But, how far have "the best of men put a different construction on the language from ourselves?" All who allow the permanency of baptism, when their minds have not been affected by controversy, have shewn, that in one important particular they did not entertain "a doubt respecting its nature;" but saw it was the design of the Saviour that it should *precede* the Lord's Supper. However they differed in other things, in this they have generally agreed; and therefore the plain question which calls their attention is, whether the institution ought, or ought not to be *excluded* from the place in which it was first appointed? In other words, ought the pattern laid before us in the New Testament, to be *regarded*, or *disregarded*.

This single enquiry if properly considered, would bring the discussion to a point. If it can be proved, that the New Testament pattern of a church is not to be copied, *both parties* will be instantly silenced. *We* shall not be able to maintain our position because we can no longer plead the authority of the Sacred volume; and *Mr. Hall*, and those baptists who adopt his theory, cannot with any show of reason plead for the baptism of believers by immersion, as an ordinance of continued obligation; for against all their arguments it will be alledged, that on their own confession, "*a new state of things has arisen;*" baptism is not requisite for its original purpose, and the *old state* of things in the primitive church, is of no force. For if it is not necessary to preserve an institution, in its primitive station, it is not possible to show, why it should be preserved at all.

Again, "we think differently of the state of the unbaptised from what the Apostles thought;"— and (he asks,") do we form the same judgment of the present Pædobaptists as the Apostles would have entertained of such as continued unbaptised in their day?" The state of the "present Pædobaptists," is not the same with that of those who refused to be baptised in the Apostles' days, for the parties stand on very different ground. The "present Pædobaptists" plead, that they *do* regard the will of Christ and the examples of the primitive Church on the very point of baptism; that they believe the law has been obeyed in their own persons, that in their view, the rite of baptism ought to be administered to infants, and that their mode of administration is according to the will of Christ. Such an opinion places them in a very different situation from those who were unbaptised in the Apostles' days, and who "refused to abide by the decision of inspired men;" and it fully justifies us in treating them as we have done. But it does not follow, that we are to accept a good man's mistake for an ordinance of Jesus Christ: nor admit that what Mr. Hall himself calls a "NULLITY," should take the place of a divine appointment in the Church of the Lord. So far as the Pædobaptists are concerned in this discussion, the question lies in narrow bounds, for if they plead that their approach to the Lord's table is regular, because they have been baptised; we answer, on this ground you cannot justly blame *us*: Baptism is a term of Communion with us *both*. If they renounce this plea, and say, baptism is *not* a term of Communion, we will meet them, in common with Mr. Hall, and ask both parties, what evidence they can produce, that the *unbaptised as such,* either ever were, or ever were designed to be, considered as members of the Christian Church, *according to the New Testament.*

In further apology for mixed communion Mr. Hall says, "*our* practice is not opposed to Apostolic precedent because that precedent respects a *different thing.*" *(p. 30.)* Had he told us how far Apostolical precedent differed from that obedience which we still owe to the command of Christ, we might have formed a judgment of his statement with more accuracy. Is baptism *now* a different thing in its *nature* and in its *end* from what it was formerly? Is it to be administered for other purposes than those which are mentioned in the New Testament? If it is, why attend to it in any instance? In that case no *Scriptural reason* can be given for regarding it, and no other is worth consideration. If Apostolic precedents are not to be viewed as interpretations of the will of Christ by which we are to be guided, we have no precedent for the baptism of any person: for precedents which respect "a different thing," from what can take place among us, are of no authority. Thus by a rapid but certain process, the Christian Church will be spared the labour of discussing one controversy, for he who takes Mr. Hall's view of the case, may avoid the trouble of inquiring into the subjects, or mode of baptism in the primitive age, since he supposes that so different is our situation from that of the early Christians, that " apostolic precedents respect *a different thing*."

Thus the debate is brought to a close; we have not a single example of baptism applicable to our circumstances; and the command of Christ, explained only by instances which have nothing in common with our situation in modern times becomes useless! An inference which inevitably follows from Mr. Hall's principles; which will be readily embraced by many; and which also clearly shows that those who plead for mixed Communion on this ground, are sacrificing to a favorite theory, an important part of their system as Baptists. That this is not their design is readily allowed, and if it is not the effect, it will be, because men's common sense will not suffer them to believe that apostolic precedents are become of no use.

It is also said, that " to be unbaptised at present is in a *moral* view a very *distinct thing* and involves very different consequences from being in that predicament in the times of the Apostles." (*Reply. p.* 29.) Mr. Hall presents this to our notice, and offers it as an alternative, that we may either deny, or affirm it, and doubtless thinks it is a dilemma from which we cannot escape. He who is unbaptised at present, from opposition to the dictates of the Apostles, we suppose will not be considered in a different moral state from the unbaptised in their day. But he who admits the permanency of baptism, who confesses that every conscientious man ought to be baptised, who believes that he has been a subject of that rite in a valid form in his infancy, is not in the situation of those who refused to obey the dictates of inspired men. *He* pleads that they have been obeyed, and if he does not mean to acknowledge that his infant baptism is unscriptural, he pleads also that their dictates were obeyed in the required order, that he was baptised before he came forward to request communion. We differ from him we acknowledge, and we do not intend to represent the point of difference as less than it has ever been, but the nature of the difference is very distinct from what it would be, if he denied the authority of the Apostles. For this reason we treat him, not as a person who designedly opposes the dictates of the Apostles, but as a mistaken good man. But still, neither will his excellencies in other parts of his character, nor our favourable opinion of him on the whole, fulfil the duty he has mistaken, or set aside our obligation to attend to the will of Christ, and support his ordinances as he delivered them. Granting, then, that on the principles now laid down, there is a difference in a moral view, between one who allows both the perpetuity and order of the first christian rite, and another who opposes apostolic authority; still it will not follow that we ought to deviate from the conduct of inspired guides. Those who do not agree in the interpretation of a law, may agree that the authority of the lawgiver demands their most respectful attention: but that is a very different thing from their uniting in a declaration, that since they vary in their interpretation, they will pursue the same course as if the law had not been enacted. Yet this is the consequence to which Mr. Hall's reasoning would conduct us.

If he could prove that the apostles required their disciples to be baptised, *not* because it was agreeable to the rule which Christ had given, but *only* because it was *then* essential to salvation, there would be more colour of probability in his reasonings; but till it is clearly demonstrated that we are not bound to adhere to the command of Christ as a *rule of conduct*, except so far as we believe it is *essential to salvation*, all that he has said against apostolic precedent is nugatory. His reasoning proceeds on the *assumption*, that the apostolic precedents were precedents only on one point, and are no authoritative guide, except when the converts of our time are in a situation similar to those of the primitive age. But if the examples in the New Testament were intended as illustrations of an institution which was to continue in force throughout all succeeding ages, we are safe in following them: and when Mr. Hall has proved, that, in the days of the apostles, there were special exemptions to the general rule, which required church members to be baptised, we will agree to admit all similar cases on that authority.

Could it be proved that baptism was in force only in apostolic times, or only in the case of those who turned from Judaism, or Heathenism to the profession of christianity (as Mr. Emlyn supposed), Mr. Hall's argument would have weight. But if baptism is an ordinance of perpetual obligation, and especially if it is the duty of every believer, as he has acknowleged it is, apostolic precedents demand every good man's attention: they bring the question home, whether he has, or has not conformed to the will of his Lord? In them he sees how it was understood and applied; they shew what was the situation of baptism in the *apostolic* church; but they will not authorise him to conclude, that he follows apostolic

E

example, if he adopts an order opposite to all that he can find in the sacred volume.

In all cases where we are left without either precept or precedent, we must act on such general principles as appear to us to be correct, and conducive to the purpose we have in view; but when we have authorised inspired precedents before us, reasoning is wasted in the attempt to shew, that we are justified in proceeding in a contrary course. For if this can be proved, a similar train of argument may be applied to other things, and we shall soon be told, that *new cases* have set aside the application of *old* rules.

SECTION III.

Mr. Hall's assertion that we assume infallibility, examined and repelled.

We are told, "that it is great presumption to claim the same deference with the apostles, and to treat those who differ from us on the sense of scripture, as though they *avowedly* opposed themselves to apostolic authority." Again—"the pædobaptists," Mr. Hall tells us, "avow their inability to discern the justice of our conclusions on the subject of baptism," and are they, he asks, "on that account, to be viewed in the same light as though they *intentionally* rejected the decision of inspired men? (*Reply p.* 20, 21.) These are strange sentiments from the pen of a Protestant Dissenter. Wherein do we "claim the same deference with the apostles? Is it in making them our guides, and in following their example? This is we grant, *deferring* to their authority, but it is *not* claiming the *same* deference with them; it is the reverse of it. That we do not view the " pædobaptists" in the same light as though they *intentionally* rejected the decision of inspired men," is evident from Mr. Hall's book. As to our treating "those who differ from us on the sense of scripture as though they *avowedly* opposed themselves to apostolic authority,"—this high sounding charge does Mr. Hall more hurt than it does us. Will he allow it, when applied to his own case, and openly confess that he treats those with whom he cannot unite, " as though they *avowedly* opposed themselves to apostolic authority"? I confess, I should be much surprised, if he did. Should he answer, that he applies it to those only who oppose communion with such as would come *to them*; this would be to *assume*, that we have no right to object to a man whose introduction into the church, would in our view, subvert the regard due to one of the institutions of Christ, and to a principle which, in our esteem, ought to be held sacred in every christian society. In his own defence, he thinks it right to say, " whether it be true or not, that we are commanded to act thus, such is our opinion, and and with this persuasion, we are not at liberty to act in a different manner." (*Reply p.* 116.) Has he a patent for the sole application of this principle? Does it belong to none but himself, and those who adopt his sentiments? He has thought proper to say, in his treatise on Terms of Communion, (*p.* 93,) that, " in the eyes of the world, who judge by sensible appearances, and are strangers to subtile distinctions, such a proceeding [as that of the strict baptists] will invariably be considered as a practical declaration, that the persons from whom *they* separate are not christians". If so, how will he clear himself from the charge, that his own conduct will invariably be considered as a practical declaration, that "churchmen from whom" *he* separates are not christians".

Further, we are charged with an assumption of *Infallibility!* We "set up a claim to inspiration, or at least to such an infallible guidance in the explanation of Scripture as is equally exempt from the danger of error or mistake: if we examine it accurately, it amounts to *more* than a claim to infallibility: it implies in the pædobaptists a knowledge of this extraordinary fact." (*Reply p.* 21.)

This is truly an absurd charge! "A claim to inspiration—to infallibility, and *more* than infallibility"! What can this mean? On this plan, there is an end of applying a rule of the New Testament to any practical purpose; for against every such application it may be said,—you claim *infallibility!* All our arguments for the independence of our churches, and for the exercise of any species of discipline on the principles of the New Testament, are open to the same reproach. Mr. Hall rejects the terms of communion in the establishment; does he therefore claim infallibility? Or, are we to conclude that he views churchmen "in the same light as though they *intentionally* rejected the decision of inspired men?" He opposes the dictates of the church of Rome, does he then assume equal infallibility? He deems the charge invalid, when applied to his own case, how then in common justice can he affix it on others? He says, (*Terms of Com. p.* 140.) the church's "cognisance of doctrine is justified by apostolic authority: a heretic after two or three admonitions reject; nor is it to any purpose to urge, the difference between ancient heretics and modern, or, that to pretend to distinguish truth from error, is a practical assumption of infallibility. While the truth of the gospel remains, a fundamental error is possible, and the difficulty of determining what is so, must be exactly proportioned to the difficulty of ascertaining the import of revelation, which he who affirms to be insurmountable, ascribes to it such an obscurity as must defeat its primary purpose." If this is correct, has the church a "cognisance of doctrine," and not of practice also? Or, does that cognisance cease, when the point in question relates to the positive precepts of the Lord? Are we justified in forming a judgement on things which affect the expulsion of an unsound member, or the refusal of an improper candidate, and are we to refrain from a practical application of what we conceive to be the direction of the Lord? Can we judge the greater matters, and not the less? If "the difficulty of ascertaining the import of revelation" be "insurmountable," respecting the manner in which members are to be admitted into the church, it will "ascribe to it such an obscurity as must defeat its primary purpose"; and thus leave us without a rule, though we have both the commission of Christ, and numerous examples which show how the apostles understood it.

If Mr. Hall's reasonings are correct, we are in a singular situation. We must not separate from others, who have (in our esteem) mistaken the will of Christ; for if we do, we are charged with treating them as though they "intentionally rejected the decision of inspired men." We must not follow what we conceive to be the clear dictates of inspiration; for this, it seems, is " to set up a claim to inspiration!" We must not conform to the directions and guidance of *infallible* men; for if we do, we claim " infallibility," and even " *more* " than infallibility!

On one occasion Mr. Hall can acknowledge that " the church is a society instituted by heaven; it is the visible seat of that kingdom which God has set up; *the laws* by which it is governed are of *his prescribing*; and the purposes which it is designed to accomplish, are limited and ascertained by infinite wisdom."(*Reply p.* 255, 256.) He goes farther still, " he who *alters* the terms of communion, changes the *fundamental laws* of Christ's kingdom. He assumes a legislative power, and ought, in order to justify that conduct, to exhibit his credentials, with a force and splendour of evidence, equal at least to those which attested the divine legation of Moses and the prophets." (*Reply p.* 255.) It seems then that the Church *has its laws, fundamental laws,* which God has *prescribed,* and which ought not to be *altered.* If so it follows, from Mr. Hall's own statement, either, that baptism never was a term of communion, or, that he who introduced the UNBAPTISED, *altered* the terms of communion, and ought to have exhibited credentials equal to those of Moses and the prophets! We certainly have not heard, that either Mr. Hall, or any of his friends, ever did bring forward such evidence; and we can therefore do no more than examine the New Testament, for the terms which are there recorded. In that volume we find that baptism *was* a term of communion; this, Mr. Hall acknowledges; we read of no alteration of terms; we therefore act on the plan there laid down. We grant, that he who *alters* the terms of communion, changes the *fundamental laws* of Christ's kingdom. This is the ground of our objection to Mr. Hall's system, which is formed on the supposition that the terms *are* altered. But, till it is proved, that the original terms are altered by the same authority by which they were enacted, we see no reason for altering our practice; and our defence is easy, for the crime alledged against us, "our enemies themselves being judges," is, that we refuse to deviate from the plan laid down by the Saviour. Whether the apostles who always themselves acted on our principle, have given authority to those who live many years afterwards to act on a *new* system, will be examined in its proper place.

SECTION IV.

Mr. Hall's concessions:—his attempt to make the Apostles parties against us.

Mr Hall has made explicit concessions respecting the fact, that the primitive converts *were* baptised *prior* to their reception into the christian church"; "the *prior claim* which baptism posseses to the attention of a christian convert," is acknowledged; he does not "contend for the propriety of inverting the *natural order* of the christian sacraments"; "it is at present the duty of the sincere believer to follow their example [that of the primitive christians] and that, supposing him to be clearly convinced of the nature and import of baptism, he would be guilty of a *criminal irregularity* who neglected to attend to it, *previous* to his entering into christian fellowship." (*Terms of Com. p.* 71, 58.) He supposes his opponent would evade one of his arguments by a distinction, and would "affirm, that though baptism *ought, agreeably to the institution of Christ, to* PRECEDE the other branches of religion, yet when it is omitted from a misconception or mistake, the omission is not of such magnitude as to prevent [the persons spoken of] from being accepted. But should our author explain himself, in this manner he will not only *coincide with us,* but his argument for strict communion will be relinquished." (*Reply p.* 83.) Let the reader weigh these concessions;—baptism has a *prior claim*"—"the *natural order* of the christian sacraments" —"a *criminal irregularity* in neglecting to attend to baptism *previous* to entering into christian fellowship"—baptism *ought, agreeably to the institution of Christ, to*

PRECEDE the other branches of religion"; What then is the inference?—That the two christian ordinances *are* connected, that the "order" in which they are arranged is so "natural," and the duty so clear that baptism "*ought* to precede other branches of religion," that even Mr. Hall is compelled to confess it. To say, that the obligation to place baptism *previous* to communion, depends on the supposition that "its nature and import" is understood, is saying nothing; its "nature and import" must exist before it can be perceived; for surely no one would say, there is no connection between the two ordinances, till a person discovers their "nature and import"; but as soon as this is understood, "he would be guilty of a "*criminal irregularity*" who neglected to attend to baptism *previous* to his entering into christian fellowship"!

The concession which our author is compelled to make, that baptism has a "prior claim" on the convert's attention, clearly shows the whole of his labour to be nothing more than an apology for setting aside a divine institution; for those whom he would introduce, he confesses are *unbaptised*, and he pleads for their admission *in that character*. So that according to his system, Jesus Christ gave a rule for the formation and regulation of his church, universal in its extent, and binding throughout all ages, but which his church ought not to maintain. However it may be covered by words that prevent its real nature from being perceived, yet the result of it is, Jesus Christ left in his church, *nominally, two* ordinances, *really*, only *one*; for the other, though acknowledged to be *his*, yet is not of sufficient consequence to be preserved in its primitive station.

On every view of the subject, there is *no doubt* of the propriety of admitting to communion a person who has been baptised, if his character and profession are consistent with the Gospel; but it is a very different thing to prove from the *New Testament*, that the title of any other person is equally clear. The way *we know* is right, will in every wise man's mind gain an instant preference; and were there no other argument than this, it would have great weight in determining him, not to hasard the adoption of a system, in which he would have all the New Testament facts against him. If however, Mr. Hall should succeed in proving, that although according to the " natural order of the christian sacraments", baptism has a " prior claim" to attention, and "*ought agreeably to the institution of Christ to precede* the other branches of religion," yet that partaking of the Lord's supper neither supposes a person "baptised nor the contrary," he might so far demolish the outworks of christianity, that there would be no security in any of its exterior appendages. The Lord's supper also might undergo any alteration which fancy might suggest; and if we attempted to appeal to the apostolic church, we should be told that " apostolic precedent respected a different thing." The same mode of argument that can remove an institution of Christ from its place, and throw it into the back ground, may effect any other change that might be desired; and the whole practice of the christian church may be put on a new footing, and modelled according to the taste of times!

Mr. Hall attempts to make the apostles parties against us. He says " we will never submit to identify two cases, which agree in nothing but the omission of an external rite, while that omission arises from causes the most dissimilar, and is combined with characters the most contrary. We will not conclude that because the apostles could not bear those that were evil, *they would have refused to tolerate the good;* or that they would have comprehended under the same censure, the contumacious opposer of their doctrines, and the *myriads of holy men* whose only crime consists in mistaking their meaning in one particular." *p,* 25, 26.

What *he* will either " not submit to," or " not

conclude," is of no consequence to us; but after we have read these high sounding words, we ask, does he then believe that the apostles would have received *the unbaptised*? If he does, where is his proof? If he does not, why does he attempt to fix a charge on us, which attaches with equal force to his own opinion? The supposition contained in the above paragraph is an impossibility, and the conclusion from it has no force. Assuming for the sake of the argument, that the apostles justified our sentiments respecting baptism, what evidence have we, that they would not have required such as had mistaken their meaning, to be baptised before they had any further connection with the church. Mr. Hall has produced none; nor have we any reason to think that candid men of any party, whose minds are not heated and warped by controversy, would ever think of denying, that the apostles would enjoin conformity to the ordinances of the gospel as they delivered them. Mr. Hall acknowledges that this was the conduct of the apostle Paul at Ephesus; when he visited that city, he found *disciples* who *believed*, and had been *baptised* unto John's baptism; yet our author pleads, that the apostle deemed their baptism invalid, and directed them to be baptised again in the name of the Lord Jesus.

"The principle of open communion" Mr. Hall says, " would have compelled us to act precisely in the same manner as the apostles did, had we been placed in their circumstances." The reason of which is, that "while there was no diversity of opinion on the subject, the voluntary omission of the baptismal ceremony could arise from nothing but a contumacious contempt of a divine precept, of which no sincere christian could be guilty." (*p.* 24, 25.) We grant, that in this case, Mr. Hall's principles as *a baptist*, would have compelled him to act as the apostles did, not in consequence of his principle of open communion, but in spite of it, since at that time there was no room for its exercise. But when the question of "opinion" is candidly examined, there is still very little "diversity" on one point, the fair consideration of which will settle the present controversy. Every one who admits the perpetuity of baptism, necessarily acknowledges, that, taking the New Testament for our guide, the members of the Church ought to be baptised. On this particular Mr. Hall and the pædobaptists agree; but here arises a difficulty; he declares *their* baptism a "NULLITY", and cannot receive them as persons who are baptised; *they* cannot come in any other character, if they believe their own declared sentiments : what then is to be done? He pleads that persons avowedly unbaptised may be received; and thus he sinks the authority of the Lord's command, and annihilates the use of apostolic precedents.

SECTION V.

Mr. Hall's misrepresentations of the statement, that Baptism is a term of christian profession, exposed.

In the chapter on "the terms of christian profession and communion pointed out in the New Testament," some expressions were used which Mr. Hall thinks he can turn to his advantage. We shall notice *the passages* which he has attacked, and then *how* he has attacked them.

The following paragraph contains three quotations, which have excited the principal part of his opposition. "In order to show that baptism is a necessary term of communion, he labours hard to prove that baptism is a term of profession. 'It is obvious,' he says, 'that their baptism [that of believers] was the term of professing their faith by the special appointment of the Lord himself.' To the same purpose, he afterwards adds, ' the fact still exists that it pleased the Lord to make a visible ritual observance, the appointed evidence of our believing in him. If obedience to a rite be not a term of Salvation (which no one supposes) yet it was ordered by the highest authority as an evidence of our subjection [submission] to the author of salvation, and a christian profession is not made *in Christ's own way* without it.' Recurring to the same topic, he observes, ' whatever may be the conditions of salvation, a plain question here occurs, which is, *ought the terms of christian communion to be different from those of christian profession?* The only answer which one would think could be given to this question would be *no*; Christian communion must require *whatever the Lord required as a mark of christian profession*'." (*Reply p.* 31, 32.) The two first of the preceding quotations are taken from ' *Baptism a term of Communion, p* 18, the third from *p.* 20.

Let any reader, of common candour and common sense, examine the expressions quoted by Mr. Hall, and let him judge, whether in the sense in which they were obviously used, they are not *true*. Take the first of them, that the baptism of the first christians " was the term of professing their faith by the special appointment of the Lord himself." With the New Testament as our guide, what other conclusion can we draw from the directions and examples which are there recorded? Can it be proved that the Lord did not require the baptism of those who professed to receive his gospel? Or, that if it was required, yet it was neither viewed by the person baptised, nor by the church that received him, as a visible, practical declaration, of his making a " christian profession" in the manner which Jesus Christ had commanded? Could these positions be demonstrated, we should be obliged, indeed, to change our ground, but this is not attempted ; on the contrary Mr. Hall confesses that " *in the apostolic age, baptism was necessary to salvation!*" *p.* 43. If so, it held a higher station than we ever ventured to assign it; and unless our author can prove, that it obtained such consequence not from the appointment of the Lord, but from some other cause, the obnoxious quotation, on his own acknowledgement, is correct.

Take the second passage, " the fact still exists, that it pleased the Lord to make a *visible* and *ritual* observance, the appointed evidence of our believing in him, &c." Let the preceding observations be applied here. If we take the New Testament for our guide, is not the proposition *true?* If it be not, let Mr. Hall disprove it. It is a fact which no candid reader of the New Testament will think of denying, that the baptism of a convert was viewed as an " evidence" of faith ; and if the perpetuity of the institution is admitted, it is an external, visible sign or evidence of faith, *still.* But if baptism is not now in its nature, what it was in its first appointment, its perpetuity is in reality denied : for in that case it is *not* the institution which the Lord appointed ; it is nothing more than a rite called by the same name, and attempted to be passed off for the same thing, but with which the primitive church was unacquainted. So evident however, is it that the institution can, and does answer the purpose already mentioned, that it is the universal sentiment expressed by those who are baptised on the profession of their faith, that baptism is their duty, as the evidence which the Lord hath appointed them to give of their submission to his authority. That this is the *only* evidence, which believers are called upon to give of their receiving, and professing the gospel, was never contended ; but that it was required on the one hand, and yielded on the other, as an evidence of faith, is too plain to be questioned. The commission and the directions which the apostles gave to the primitive converts show this fully; and the appeal which the apostle Paul makes to his brethren at Rome, sets forth the subject in a forcible manner. "Know ye not, that so many of you as were baptised into Jesus Christ were baptised into his death? Therefore we are buried with him by baptism into death; that like as Christ, was raised up from the dead by the glory of the Father, even so, we also should walk in newness of life." *Rom.* vi 3—4. In this impressive passage, the apostle appeals to the baptism of the believers at Rome, as an acknowledged evidence that they knew the ends answered by the death and resurrection of the Lord: not only that they believed the facts, but the doctrine exhibited by the facts; and "therefore" in consequence of their faith, and as a solemn declaration of it, they were "buried with him by baptism unto death". Such was the case with christians of old: and the inquiry naturally follows, whether *our* profession, and *our* baptism ought, or ought not to resemble theirs. If obedience to the baptismal ceremony was *not* "ordered by the highest authority as an evidence of our submission to the author of salvation," let it be proved, either that baptism was not designed for this end, or that it is not a permanent institution. It was also stated, that a christian profession is not made "*in Christ's own way*" without baptism. If this be an error, if Christ did *not* require a profession to be made *in this manner*, let the error be shown. This however is not attempted.

The third quotation is of the same nature with the preceding; the words are used in the same sense and it is capable of the same defence. Of the term "profession", we shall soon have occasion to speak more particularly. Of baptism as "a mark of christian profession," we shall only observe, that when Mr. Hall has *proved*, that baptism was NOT *required as a mark of christian profession*, we will agree no longer to defend the paragraph.

It now remains to be shewn *how* Mr. Hall *has attacked these passages.*

He begins by taking new ground; he now says, "we freely acknowledge that if the principle can be established, that baptism is *invariably essential* to a christian profession, the cause we are pleading must be abandoned, being confident that a *true profession* of the christian religion is inseparable from church communion." *p.* 32, 33. Again, "now that the profession of Christ is an *indispensible term of salvation,* is so undeniably evident from the New Testament, that to attempt to prove it, seems like an insult on the understanding of the reader." *p.* 34. Here he conducts the unwary reader, to a proposition of a very different nature from any thing that we have stated. The substance of what we had alledged was, that according to the New Testament, baptism was required at our entrance on a visible profession, as a testimony of faith in Christ, and of devotedness to him; and for this reason, we called it the " term" and "mark of christian profession," Mr. Hall leads the reader's attention from this object, and insinuates that we make baptism essential to the christian character; that "the necessary inference is the restriction of the hope of future happiness to members of our own denomination"; and that "the pædobaptists are on our principles cut off from the hope of eternal life, and salvation is confined to ourselves." (*p.* 36.) Since it is manifest that we never advanced such opinions as these, the reader may ask, on what ground they are so confidently charged upon us? The answer is, on the application which Mr. Hall *now* thinks proper to make of the term *profession.* Time was, when he could use it in the sense in which it has been commonly understood among baptists, and in which sense we had used it. He could on a former occasion, speak of " such as professed their faith in Christ under the ministry of the apostles", as persons who "were *baptised on that profession."* He could tell us, that "the *profession required* in a candidate for christian baptism involved a historical faith, a belief in a certain individual, an illustrious personage, &c." He could speak of " the *profession* demanded in the baptism of John", and distinguish it from "the faith required by the apostles"; he called John's baptism " the rite intended to anounce the future, though speedy appearance of the Messiah", and christian baptism, " the ceremony *expressive of a firm belief* in an identical person, as already manifested under that illustrious character." He could then say, when giving reasons why the disciples of the Lord were not baptised with what he calls christian baptism, that "such as had *professed* their faith in Christ from the period of his first manifestation, could not without palpable incongruity *recommence that profession.*" "By orthodox christians it is uniformly maintained that union to Christ is formed by faith, and as the baptists are distinguished by demanding *a profession of it at baptism,* they are at least precluded from asserting that rite to have any concern in effecting the spiritual alliance in question." (*Terms of Com. p.* 38, 19, 20, 21, 42, 119.) These passages fully show, that Mr. Hall could *once* acknowledge, that there was a correct sense in which a profession of faith was required, and was given at baptism. But *now* he quotes a number of texts in which the words *confession* and *profession* occur, (which he tells us are of the same meaning) and he charges us with the inferences he thinks fit to draw from them, as if we were bound to deny the christianity of those, who differed from us in their view of the manner in which such a profession ought to be visibly expressed.

But, if his argument proves any thing, it proves too much; for according to his own acknowledgement, the baptism of the primitive converts *was* the *commencement* of their *profession*; so that all the passages he quotes, in which the words *profession* and *confession* are used, relate to persons who were baptised, and who made their profession at their baptism; and when these passages were written, he acknowledges that *baptism was essential to their salvation.* On his own system therefore, either he and the sacred writers mean different things by the same word, or the force of his argument is against himself; for there is not a single inspired writer who enforces the necessity of a christian profession, who did not mean a profession visibly made by baptism. But Mr. Hall does *not* mean a profession made by baptism; since, in his view, baptism either may or may not be included in it. If however, during the period of inspiration baptism was always a part of christian profession, it remains with *him* to explain, how that ordinance, which he tells us was once essential to salvation, is now dwindled into such insignificance, that it is not to be retained in the church in its original station, and, that " communion neither supposes a person baptised, nor the contrary!" So that according to his view of the subject, the religion of the primitive church has undergone a complete alteration; baptism does not answer its original purpose, and profession means a different thing now, from what it did in the time of the Apostles!

We expressly stated, that we did not consider obedience *to a rite* to be a *term of salvation.* In our estimation therefore, baptism did not hold the same place that " profession" does in the estimation of Mr. Hall; for he says that " the profession of Christ is an indisputable term of salvation". His design, however, is to involve us in the charge of making these two the same thing, in direct opposition to the statement already mentioned; for the whole of his reasoning depends on the supposition, that we affirmed *obedience to a rite* to be essential to what he now calls a *"profession".* He says, the argument which we urged " turns on the principle that baptism is a term of christian profession". (*p.* 36.) True; but in what sense?—that baptism was the appointed, visible manner in which Christ directed the christian professor to testify his faith in him: and can Mr. Hall deny this? We never imagined that good men might not through prejudice or misapprehension mistake the directions of the New Testament; we explicitly acknowledged this, and therefore placed our argument on a basis common to the great body of professing christians. But when the inquiry concerns the obedience due to institutions, which in their nature are external and visible things, and in which we can have no guide but positive law, the question then is, what are the directions of the New Testament concerning them? If Jesus Christ *did* require baptism in the visible profession of faith in him, and prior to a regular connection with his church; and if the institution was designed to be perpetual, we must either say, *his* having required it *is* a rule for us; or, the directions which he has given us are so *defective* that they are insufficient for our guidance. Mr. Hall may take which he pleases; the first destroys his system, the second exposes its true nature.

It also deserves attention, that all our observations on this part of the subject, were drawn to a point in one comprehensive, "obvious *principle;*" which is that "baptism was intended to be a visible evidence of connection with the christian church". (*Baptism a term of Com. p.* 21.) This principle of itself, (and especially when taken with the explanation given of it) is a complete contradiction to Mr. Hall's inferences; and the terms in which it is couched shew that the system for which we pleaded, had no alliance with those violent charges which stain his pages. The principle is brought to a practical issue, and when he has said all he can, a calm inquirer will perceive, that the whole argument hinges on the truth or falsehood of this principle. If it is false, let its falsehood be proved; and let it be shown what the institution was intended for. But if it be true, all that we ask is, that the ordinance be regarded for its designed purpose. Here however, Mr. Hall has deserted the field. Far from meeting the argument, he leaves his readers without information whether baptism answers any important purpose; or whether it is not an antiquated ordinance of little authority, and less utility.

The "position" that the terms of communion and of salvation are the same, was briefly examined in our former work, p. 19—20. We denied its accuracy, and stated a few queries and observations, as difficulties arising from the position. Part of these remarks Mr. Hall quotes;— he calls them extraordinary and intreats the reader to "*pause and meditate*"! "The design of producing them at present", we are told, "is to shew the tendency of the principle"; and the reader is requested to consider "whether they are susceptible of any other sense than that the terms of salvation and of communion are commensurate with each other". (*p.* 38.) But if any of our readers should suppose this, after he has read the paragraph from which the extracts are taken, we should either be sorry for his prejudices or lament his incapacity.

One of the difficulties arising from the "position" already mentioned was, "if baptism was *once* necessary to communion, either it was then essential to salvation, or that which was not essential to salvation, was essential to communion? To this Mr. Hall replies, "that in the apostolic age, baptism *was necessary to salvation*". (*p.* 43.) A query then succeeded, "if it [baptism] was *then* essential to salvation, how can it be proved not to be essential *now*"? To this our author says, "it is unnecessary to attempt it, because it is admitted by Mr. K. himself; and it is preposterous to attempt the proof of what is acknowledged by both parties". p. 43. This is *evading* the inquiry, not answering it. It would *not* have been "preposterous" for Mr. Hall to have shewn *how, when,* and by *what means,* a duty still obligatory, and once *essential* to salvation, now occupies, according to his system, a situation so depressed, that it is made to give way to every opinion which intrudes on its original claims. Instead of doing this, he attempts to remove from his own system the weight which pressed upon it, by saying, " the difficulty attending the supposition of a change in the terms of salvation, is urged with little propriety, by one to whose hypothesis they apply in their full force". (*p.* 44.) If he means that on *our "hypothesis"* "a change in the terms of salvation" has taken place, he shews that he does not understand it. Far from entangling ourselves in speculations about variable essentials, or attempting to determine in what circumstances a duty might, or might not be essential to salvation, we took the New Testament account, and on the supposition that it was allowed to be our guide, we pleaded the authority of its directions, its examples, and its general principles. After we had explicitly stated that *obedience to a rite* no one supposed was a term of salvation, and then opposed Mr. Hall's "position", that the terms of communion and of salvation were the same, we shall leave the reader to judge with what consistency he attempts to press this "difficulty" upon us. The fact is, it attaches exclusively to *his* hypothesis. If he *can* prove that *anciently* men were saved on one "*condition*", but *now* are saved on another, let him do so; but if he cannot, the inference which we urged against him, continues in all its force.

After all, he grants that " owing to the *incurable ambiguity* of language, many truths founded on the clearest evidence assume an appearance of *paradox;* and of this nature is the proposition which affirms that the terms of salvation are not unalterable: which may with equal propriety be affirmed and denied in different senses". (*p.* 44.) There is then on his own confession, a sense in which all that he pleads for may be "denied" with quite as much propriety as he has thought proper to "affirm" it. In the next page he is compelled to confess, that "there are certain doctrines which are revealed because they are *necessary;* and others which are necessary *only because they are revealed."*

Of this nature, he informs us, are "the few and simple ceremonies" of the Gospel. (*p.* 45.) We are then told that on its first publication, "the visible appendages of christianity were exhibited with a lustre of evidence, which no honest mind could withstand; and that no pretence for their neglect could subsist among such as possessed religious integrity. Such was eminently the case with the two institutions which have occasioned the present controversy". (*p.* 46.) Admitting for the sake of argument that this was the case, if the decease of the Apostles has lessened "the lustre of evidence" with which the "visible *appendages* of christianity were exhibited," it has produced the same effect on them all; and, however much they have lost the "lustre" of their evidence, the directions of the Lord and the practical explanations given us in the conduct of inspired men are still visible. If these continue in our bibles for any useful purpose, the least that they can be supposed to answer is, to form the rule of our conduct; but if we are not to follow them as our rule, we have no rule. This is the issue to which Mr. Hall would conduct us, for all his reasonings are nothing more than *excuses for* NOT *following the Apostles and the primitive church!* We do not pretend to say what may, or may not in all cases consist with "religious integrity", or how far evidence must be carried before it can be asserted that "*no* honest mind can withstand it"; but if it be granted that baptism and the Lord's supper were "the visible appendages of christianity", but that *now* the unbaptised ought to be admitted into the church, how can a man of plain common sense avoid the conclusion, that on this system, one of these "visible appendages" is set aside. We anticipate the reply, that, once it was indispensable as a "*visible* appendage", because it was *then* necessary to salvation, but it is not so *now*. An apology of no weight, unless the obligation to attend to baptism ceased when it became *not* necessary to salvation.

But whether it *is* or is *not* necessary to eternal happiness, unless it is repealed, it is still the command of the Lord, and has the same appointed station in his church it ever had. This is the plain reason why we should submit to it, and preserve it in its place; and this argument retains all its force, however the speculations of men, respecting either the ancient or the present consequence of the institution, may terminate.

To sum up all that we think necessary on the subject of *essentials*, we allow in the words of Mr. Hall, that "union to Christ is formed by faith", and that the "baptists are distinguished by demanding a *profession* of it at baptism". We grant therefore his conclusion, that we are "precluded from asserting that rite to have any concern in effecting the spiritual alliance in question". (*Terms of Com. p.* 119. 120.) On this ground we say, strictly speaking, baptism never was essential to salvation; for whatever is essential takes place in all good men. Without union to Christ by faith, we do not conceive *any* man can be saved, but we know no one who will say the same thing concerning baptism. In the instances on record in the New Testament, baptism was the effect of professing to receive the truth in the love of it: such a reception of the truth, we allow *was* essential to salvation, and obedience to the will of Christ arose from it. We allow that no good man would refuse submitting to this part of the Lord's will in the days of the Apostles, and we maintain that no such person who believes in the perpetuity of baptism can now deny, that *according to the New Testament* all professing believers ought to be baptised, and that they cannot consistently come to the Lord's table except in that character. Whether therefore he agrees with us respecting the proper mode and subjects of baptism or not, he is compelled to act on our general principle. But if he solicits communion with us on the ground of his infant baptism, he asks us to admit the validity of that ceremony. If he requests us to admit him as unbaptised, he then asks that we would join with him in practically denying what both confess is the will of Christ; for both admit that church members ought to be baptised; yet *we* are to receive a person who is *unbaptised*, and *he* agrees to be accepted under that character! Should he say, I acknowledge the propriety of the general rule, but I wish you would consider my case as an exception: we reply, so we will, provided you can show, either that such an exception is to be found in the New Testament, or that we need not be guided by that volume. In few words, we consider baptism not essential to salvation in the proper meaning of the terms; but it is essential to correct obedience, and to the testimony of a good conscience, in every instance in which the permanency of the institution is admitted. Whoever therefore, apprehends that he is unbaptised, should give this subject a serious consideration; for though some men of whom we hope well, deceive themselves by inconsistent reasonings, yet it is the plain rule of God's word, and not a good man's irregularities that ought to be our guide.

Mr. Hall thinks proper to represent us as stating, "that the limits of communion must be the same with those of profession; that *the Pædobaptists have none, or at least none that is valid*"; and that on *this* account, and for *this* reason, they are precluded from a title to christian fellowship". (*p.* 38—39.) The expression "a christian profession is not made in Christ's own way" without baptism, he takes more than usual pains to torture; and says, the scope of our argument obliged us to "prove that *adult baptism* is essential to a christian profession:" but we are now content "with saying that without that ordinance, it is not made in the right way". He then twists the words till he supposes they mean "perfect profession", and after declaring that this is not "the lot of a mortal", he adds, "but though this is the only interpretation *consistent with truth,* we cannot for a moment suppose that such was the meaning of the writer. He *must have intended to assert,* that the parties to whom they are applied, fail to make what Christ himself would deem a profession". A number of consequences are then deduced by Mr. Hall, and the conclusion is, that our reasoning "will consign the Pædobaptists to destruction"! (*p.* 39—42.) To these charges and the rest of the same class, a reference to the work from which they are taken is all that is necessary. Let the reader examine the argument as it was originally stated, and then let him form his own conclusions.

As to the expression "a christian profession is not made in Christ's own way without baptism ;" if the reader observes the words which immediately follow it, he can then judge whether Mr. Hall's inferences are correct. "It is now too late to say, this is not what the New Testament has enjoined; and it does not become us to alter what *is enacted* by infinite wisdom. There may be, and there are, differences of opinion respecting the subjects and mode of baptism : but as the ordinance itself was prescribed by the Lord, it ought to be visibly recognised in his Church". (*Baptism &c. p.* 18, 19.)

Whether our mode of reasoning, which was placed on a basis common to all that admit the perpetuity of baptism, did consign "the Pædobaptists to destruction," is easily determined. Whatever were its defects *that* is not fairly to be charged upon it. After having guarded our statement, by saying that we did *not* esteem obedience to a rite a term of salvation, but that we considered it as "an evidence of our submission to the author of salvation"; after having explicitly declared, that the Baptists "do not consider baptism necessary to salvation; they do not depend upon it for their acceptance before God ; nor do they view any as fit subjects for that ordinance, who are not *previously* believers in Christ, and justified in the sight of God by their faith"; (*Baptism a term of Com. p.* 31.) we need not say any thing farther in reply to Mr. Hall's arguments on this part of the controversy. They have nothing to do with the subject as we stated it; and they are founded on such complete misrepresentations, that we are not involved in their consequences.

Since however, he has thought proper to notice some expressions which we made use of, and to investigate what he calls their "meaning", we also shall notice one thing intimately connected with them which *he* has omitted. We need not repeat what has been already observed respecting the sense in which "baptism is a term of profession", nor is it necessary to defend the terms we have used, if they are taken in their connection. They all had a relation to the visible, designed end of baptism. But what says Mr. Hall on this part of the subject? NOTHING. Yet if baptism continues in force, it must be designed to answer some intelligible purpose. We ask then, if it is *not* a visible profession of faith in Christ, if it is *no evidence of connection* with the Christian church, if a profession of our faith *is* made in the way which Christ required without baptism; *what is its use,* and *on what ground does it now claim any attention?*

SECTION VI.

The difference of sentiment among Christians respecting the doctrine of Election—the prohibition to eat blood— and the imposition of hands on the baptised—examined as to their supposed bearing on this controversy.

In the progress of his work, Mr. Hall reminds us of the difference of sentiments among christians on the doctrine of Election, some taking the Calvinistic and others the Arminian view of it. We are informed that such a difference of opinion could not exist in the primitive church; and that " were these parties to exclude each other from communion under the pretence that the primitive christians were all Calvinists, or all Arminians," they would reason in the same manner that we do. (*Reply p.* 48, 49.) He adds, "how would our author repel this reasoning, or justify a more liberal conduct? He certainly cannot allege the original obscurity of the apostolic injunctions, and the possibility of primitive converts mistaking their meaning: he would *unquestionably* insist on the different degrees of importance attached to revealed truths, and the palpable difference between mistaking the meaning, and avowedly opposing the sentiments, of inspired writers. *But this is precisely our mode of defence.*" (*p.* 49.)

He is however altogether mistaken; we should not think of placing the decision of the ultimate question, whether Calvinists and Arminians might hold fellowship together on such a ground as this; we should appeal to the New Testament respecting the terms on which persons ought to be received to baptism. If we ought to be baptised into a creed which is to include all that is supposed to be taught in the New Testament, it would be right to examine whether it was an Arminian creed or a Calvinistic creed, and then the question would be of high importance, into which creed shall we be baptised. But if we derive our information from the sacred volume, we find, that the proper subjects of baptism, ought to be baptised on a profession of their faith in Christ as the Son of God, and the saviour of sinners. Whatever any person considers as necessarily and essentially included in believing in Christ, he must, we grant, make a term of communion, because in his view, it is a necessary part of the confession which a candidate ought to make at his baptism. On this ground, he who conceives the Calvinistic view of the doctrine of election, *essential to a person's faith in Christ*, must make Calvinism a term of communion; and so on the opposite side of the question, he who believes that the Calvinistic sentiment is inconsistent with faith in Christ, must necessarily exclude Calvinists from church fellowship. " Orthodox christians" Mr. Hall informs us, consider " the explicit belief of the doctrine of the atonement" indispensably necessary to salvation. He also says, that the immediate followers of Christ did not embrace this truth. It seems that this is given as an instance of a *new* essential arising in the church. " The full development of the gospel scheme, made at a subsequent period, has in this instance rendered that essential to salvation, which could previously subsist without it."*(p. 46.)* Suppose that this view of the subject is correct, the reason why the belief of the doctrine of the atonement is *now* necessary to salvation is, because it comes within the limits of the direction " he that *believeth* and is baptised shall be saved." Whatever is an essential part of a reply to the question," dost thou believe on the Son of God," we acknowledge is a term of communion; because it is, according to the New Testament, a term of baptism. Such were the constitutional principles of the church in the purest ages, when every thing was regulated by *unerring inspiration*. If it can be proved that its constitution is not *now* what it was *originally*, we must change our ground ; but till that is done, we need not tremble for the ultimate success of our cause.

An attempt it made to perplex the question before us, by bringing in the decision of the Apostles and Elders at Jerusalem prohibiting the eating of blood in Acts xv. Mr. Hall selects this part of the decision of the Apostolical Council, without at all noticing the difficulties attending the passage at large ; though he must know, that it has greatly divided the most learned and acute Commentators. It seems to us, that the view given of the decision recorded in this chapter by the learned SPENCER is rational, and supported by very strong evidence ; that the reason why the Gentile Christians were required to " abstain from pollutions of idols, and from fornication, and from things strangled, and from blood," (*Acts* xv. 20,) was, because these things were " the causes, the attendants, and the signs of Idolatry."* Whoever, therefore, was defiled by these practices, was to be considered as sanctioning Idolatry, and equally opposing the religion of Moses and of Christ. He who in these things symbolized with Idolaters, would be excluded from the communion of the christian church ; or if he had not been received into the church, for the same reason he would not be admitted to baptism. Such practices would be considered as proving that the man was a Heathen, and while he continued such, he could not be received into the christian community. But Mr. Hall selects the prohibition of blood as an article of food, which he affirms was once a term of communion, and he says that " the precept of abstaining from blood, was *invariably observed by the faithful* from the time of Noah." (*Reply, p.* 50.)

---

* Vide Dissert. in Act. xv, 20, Cap. III. § i, at the end of the second book of his work, *De legibus ritualibus Hebræorum*.

Nay further, he says, "I have not the smallest doubt, that it is of perpetual force, however little it may be regarded in modern practice." (*p.* 50.) For the sake of consistency then, he ought not to admit into the number of "*the faithful*" any man who, in his estimation, violates this precept; and if he does not mean to say, that positive precepts are of no force, he ought to reject such a person from a participation of Christian ordinances.

He seems to consider the precept given to Noah, and the advice of the apostles to the Gentile christians respecting abstinence from blood, as the same. He thinks proper to put this advice, on a par with the injunction concerning baptism. He acknowledges that the "precept respecting blood was not promulgated by the Saviour himself; but resulted from the solemn and unanimous decision of his apostles, and is of more ancient origin than *any other christian institute.*" (*Reply p.* 51.) Here a supposed prohibitory precept is called a *christian institute,* and is said to be of more ancient origin than any *other* christian institute. It seems then, that this *christian* institute, is far older than christianity itself. But leaving the reader to settle this point in the best way he can, we are further told, that "there is no room to allege a misapprehension of the meaning of the precept; it is susceptible but of one interpretation." (*Reply p.* 50.) This is a mistake: Jewish writers understand the precept given to Noah to mean, that he was not to eat the blood, with the flesh of the animal while it was alive, by cutting off any part and instantly using it for food, before the creature was properly slain. This barbarous custom was not only practised anciently, but is still in use in some parts of the World. It is remarkable that the *Jews,* who have been always distinguished for their abhorrence of blood, should have given this interpretation of the precept, and they seem to have been led to it, by an accurate attention to Hebrew phraseology. Dr. GILL, whose extensive acquaintance with Jewish literature cannot be denied, says, "it is the *constant sense* of the Jewish synagogue, that this law is to be understood of the member of a living creature torn from it and eaten whilst alive." *(Expos. on Acts* xv. 29.) Many christian writers of distinguished eminence have adopted the same sentiment. Hence they have drawn a clearly marked line of distinction between the precept given to Noah,—the ceremonial precepts given to the Jews,—and the advice given by the apostles to the Gentile christians. They have shewn that in their estimation, the first and the two last, related to different things; and that the precepts given to the Jews, and the advice of the apostles were distinguished from each other by two important circumstances; that the precepts of Moses were absolute, and binding on every member of the Jewish dispensation; but that the directions given by the apostles, arose from the peculiar state of the church, and did not mark the precepts respecting meats offered to idols, things strangled, and blood, as universally and perpetually binding.

Whoever will take the trouble to examine the writings of our most learned christian commentators and critics, will see that there is not that uniformity which will warrant Mr. Hall's assertion, that "there is no room to allege a misapprehension of the meaning of the precept; it is susceptible but of one interpretation". *(p.* 50.)

I am no advocate for eating blood; but since the precept given to Noah which Mr. Hall supposes has a relation to this practice, is unnecessarily forced upon our attention, the reader will, I hope, pardon one observation more which may tend to elucidate that precept. We read in the law of Moses, "Ye shall not eat of any thing that *dieth of itself;* thou shalt give it unto the stranger that is in thy gates, THAT HE MAY EAT IT, or thou mayest sell it unto an alien". *Deut.* xiv. 21. If an animal *died of itself,* the blood was still in the system, and the flesh could not be eaten without eating the blood also, as is the case with animals that are strangled; but though Israelites might not eat such food, strangers were permitted to eat it even *by the Law of God.* How then can Mr. Hall prove that the precept prohibiting " the use of blood in food", " was enjoined expressly on the Gentiles",—and, " was in force from the period of the deluge ?" (*p.* 49. 50.) If his sense of the precept is correct, it is inconceivable that such a permission as that which is recorded in the law of Moses, should have been given : and if he fails in establishing the universal obligation of the precept according to his interpretation of it, during the time of the Jewish dispensation, he will not find it an easy task, to establish its universal and perpetual obligation under the dispensation of the gospel. Besides, the prohibition of blood stands on the same basis with that of " meats offered to idols", but it is certain that the eating of meat offered to idols, was not universally unlawful ; it therefore follows of course that in the present case, the decision of the apostles will not of itself prove the prohibition of blood to be universally, and permanently binding.

But the end our author has in view, is to press an imaginary difficulty on us, from the comparison which he thinks proper to draw, between the injunction which *prohibited* blood, and that which *commanded* baptism. " As Pædobaptists profess their conscientious adherence to the baptismal precept, which they merely demand the right of interpreting for themselves ; upon what principle is it, that a mistake in the meaning of a positive injunction, is deemed more criminal than its avowed neglect; or why should an error in judgment which equally affects the practice in both cases, be tolerated it in the one, and made the ground of exclusion in the other ?" (*Reply p.* 51, 52.) The answer to this is easy :—he who believes that a precept of a former dispensation, is of so great authority *at present*, that obedience to it *now*, ought to be required by a christian church, must make it a term of baptism, and of course a term of communion. But he who considers it not supported by such evidence as gives it this importance, though he may individually think it right, does not feel himself compelled to insist upon it. He therefore, can retort Mr. Hall's argument; and since the "very pith and marrow" of his "cause" is, that *baptism* is not necessary to communion, such a person in his turn may ask, "upon what principle is it, that a mistake in the meaning of a positive injunction not belonging to the christian dispensation, should be deemed of equal consequence with the "*avowed neglect*" of an ordinance peculiar to that dispensation? Mr. Hall attempts to place the injunction against eating blood, on the same level with the command which enjoins baptism, and hence the inference unavoidably follows, that, according to his mode of reasoning, baptism is of no more consequence than the precept against eating blood! The effect of such a mode of lowering a christian ordinance, is easily seen; and will be very agreeable to many; for it will afford them an excellent excuse for neglecting, what they do not wish to obey.

In addition to what our author has alleged concerning the eating of blood, he thinks proper to say, "the argument equally applies to laying on of hands after ordination and baptism. It is acknowledged that this rite was universally practised in the primitive times, that it claims the sanction of apostolic example, and it is enumerated by St. Paul among the *first principles* of christian doctrine". (*Reply* p. 52.)

That imposition of hands took place after baptism when an apostle was present, and when miraculous gifts were conferred, is acknowledged; that it was used as a necessary appendage to baptism, when an apostle was *not* present, and when extraordinary gifts were *not* given, has not been proved; and we believe cannot be proved.

When Mr. Hall has demonstrated that imposition of hands was constantly practised by apostolic authority in cases where spiritual gifts were not conferred—so that this usage was a regular part of christian baptism; when he has proved, that apostles directed those who had no spiritual gifts to bestow, to use the imposition of hands after baptism, and that the christian ordinance was considered incomplete without it; *then,* but not *till then,* will his argument have any force. As to the imposition of hands after ordination, it is so distant from the present enquiry, that it may be dismissed as wholly irrelevant*.

It is not a little remarkable, that Mr. Hall should urge two arguments, taken from passages concerning which the christian world has been much divided, and apply them as if their sense was clear and undisputed. To explain that which is difficult, by what is clear and undisputed is rational ; but to perplex what is plain, by that which is difficult and uncertain, cannot promote the cause of truth.

* The following note of Dr. Doddridge on Heb. vi. 2. deserves attention:

" *The imposition of hands.*] This answered such great purposes in the christian church, as the appointed method of communicating important gifts, that it might well be mentioned among *first principles.* But it is by a very precarious consequence, that any can infer from hence the *universal* obligation of this rite, in admitting persons into full *church-membership,* or even to the *ministry. See Pierce's Vindication,* p. 463.

Family Expositor."

SECTION VII.

Mr. Hall's criticisms on the use of the term "evidence" examined—He does not recognise the scriptural design of baptism; and his system subverts the institution.

Two expressions are next selected from 'Baptism a term of communion,' which Mr. Hall calls "remarkable passages" (*Reply p.* 53.); the first has been noticed already; the next I suppose is taken from p. 30: both are brought forward because the term *evidence* occurs in them.

The latter Mr. Hall quotes imperfectly; in his book it is "the appointed *evidence* of our putting on Jesus Christ": the original words are, "the *first, visible,* appointed evidence of our putting on Jesus Christ".

Our author begins his scrutiny by saying, "let us first ascertain the *precise meaning* of these remarkable passages"; —but how? By viewing " these remarkable passages" in their connection, by observing the terms which are used, by comparing the paragraphs where the same or similar expressions are employed, for the purpose of discovering the common sentiment which runs through the whole? No; this common place way of examining a subject is far from Mr. Hall's method; he plays on the term *evidence,* turns it into a variety of shapes, at last having found one which he thinks will answer his purpose, he declares that this must be its "*precise meaning*"! Observe his mode of discussion. The "meaning *must be*, that the ordinance in question forms a necessary *part* of the evidence *of faith,* insomuch that in the absence of it our Lord intended no other should be deemed valid." He then adds, "that this was the case in the primitive age, we feel no hesitation in affirming." (*Reply. p.* 54.)

Let the reader compare our statements with Mr. Hall's inference. In the first of the passages quoted, we said "if obedience to a rite be *not* a term of salvation (*which no one supposes*), yet it was ordered by the highest authority as an evidence of our subjection to the author of salvation". In this sentence, the supposition laid down is, that obedience to a rite is *not* a term of salvation. The parenthesis which follows "(*which no one supposes*)", clearly shows, that we neither intended to argue on the ground that baptism was an evidence of faith essential to salvation, nor did we imagine that we had to contend with any one upon that ground. Here then we ask, on what pretence could it be inferred that the "precise meaning" of the first of "these remarkable passages, *must be*, that the ordinance in question forms a necessary part of the evidence of faith, insomuch that in the absence of it, our Lord intended no other should be deemed valid"; since the passage itself contains a distinct denial of our author's inference?

Further, in the short paragraph from whence Mr. Hall makes his second quotation, baptism was denominated "the *first, visible*, appointed evidence of our putting on Jesus Christ. Gal. iii. 27." Here again, let any one judge whether, in fair interpretation, Mr. Hall's inference can be drawn from the words used, for he has quoted them so inaccurately, that we do not refer to his quotation. On the question, whether the Lord will deem no evidence of faith valid, if baptism be absent, this statement offers no opinion; and what it asserts, our opponent is at full liberty to disprove as soon as he is able. A duty may be required, as a visible evidence of subjection to Christ, without its being supposed that its absence in any case, or a mistake which may be made concerning it, would subject a man to eternal condemnation. That this is not our sentiment is evident even from the "remarkable passages" which Mr. Hall quotes; yet notwithstanding, he thinks fit to assert, that the contrary must be their "*precise meaning!*"

The sense which Mr. Hall attempts to affix on our words, he confesses expressed the true state of things in the primitive age; but it seems that what was true *then*, is not true *now*. We are charged with making baptism "a necessary part of the evidence of faith, insomuch that in the absence of it, our Lord intended no other should be deemed valid." Mr. Hall adds, "*That this was the the case in the primitive age, we feel no hesitation in affirming.*" (*p.*54.) So that all we had said was, on Mr. Hall's confession, a *correct* state of the case in the days of the Apostles, and according to the accounts given in the New Testament.

In his progress, Mr. Hall quotes half a sentence from p. 67 of 'Baptism a term of Communion'; had he quoted the whole, especially had he taken it in its connection, every one would have seen that it did not suit his purpose. But now he grows bolder than before, and we are accused of the inconsistency of admitting the piety of those "who are destitute of that which Jesus Christ prescribed as THE evidence of faith." (*Reply p.* 55.) The next thing is a quotation from another place (*p.* 140), taken also in his manner, neither noticing the design, nor the explanation given of the words; and then he finishes the paragraph by talking about " palpable contradictions."

But the view which we have given of our sentiments on this subject is before the world; with those who are not convinced, on comparing our statements with Mr. Hall's interpretations, that instead of ascertaining our "precise meaning," he has laboured to affix to our words *precisely* what they were never designed to mean, we shall not contend—the interests of truth are not likely to be promoted by striving with persons of that description.

According to Mr. Hall's reasoning, our former arguments are of no force, unless it could be demonstrated that baptism "*occupies the same place at present, and that it is* STILL *necessary to constitute a valid evidence of faith in the Redeemer."* (*Reply p.* 54.) This brings forward an inquiry of vital importance to the present controversy, which our author has most completely neglected; and that is, *what place does baptism* NOW *occupy?* If it occupies the same place it did in apostolic times, his system is ruined by his own confession. If it occupies a *different* place, what is that place? What was the design of baptism? Is it now a *"different thing"* from what it was in the days of inspiration? On this subject Mr. Hall is prudently silent. Whatever the design of baptism was, the institution ought either to be administered for the purpose first appointed, or it cannot be maintained as a New Testament ordinance. If baptism ought not to be continued for its primitive purpose, the sooner we lay it aside the better; for we cannot pretend to practise it on scriptural authority. We can have no idea of the perpetuity of an institution, when its ends are no longer answered. Whenever this is the case, " it decayeth and waxeth old," and " is ready to vanish away."

Here then the question comes to a point; it must either be disproved, or acknowledged, that we ought *now* to baptise for the same reasons as the apostles baptised. If they administered this ordinance for *one* reason, but we ought to administer it for *another*, where is this twofold set of reasons to be discovered? If it be proved that the same ends are not answered by the institution, and the same reasons do not now apply that were in force in the days of inspiration, then the *scriptural* reasons for its administration are given up; it is no longer the baptism of the New Testament; it is nothing more than a superstitious ceremony, and has no more claim on our attention than an abrogated Jewish rite. But, if it must be *acknowledged* that we ought still to administer baptism for the reasons assigned in the New Testament—all we ask is, that the inspired rule be followed, and the present controversy will instantly terminate.

But the difference between the state of things now, and in the age of inspiration, has brought forward "a new case;" so that baptism does not occupy "the same place" it once did! Whatever difference of circumstances has taken place, is the rule invalidated, or does it still continue as a rule? If it is admitted that baptism was essential to salvation in the days of the apostles, to the whole extent of Mr. Hall's idea, and that the circumstances of the times *then* gave it peculiar importance, yet nothing is more clear than that our reasonings and conduct should be guided by the rule which is *permanent*, and not by those circumstances which from their nature could be only *temporary*. If then, we take the New Testament for our guide, how are we to admit the *unbaptised*, unless we either plead for " inverting the *natural order* of the christian sacraments;" or, suppose that the directions given us are not urged with legislative authority, but are only *general advice*, submitted to our prudence, and left to our inclination?

Mr. Hall denies, that baptism was "more *specifically* intended as a test of faith than compliance with any other part of the mind of Christ; or that it was *in any other sense* an evidence of that attainment, than as it was necessary to evince the possession of christian sincerity." (*Reply p.* 54.) To the first of these assertions we reply, our statement was *not* that baptism was "more *specifically* intended as a test of faith than compliance with any other part of the mind of Christ;" but that it was "the first, visible, appointed evidence, of our putting on Jesus Christ." If this is not agreeable to the New Testament, let it be disproved. As to the second assertion, suppose for the sake of the argument that we admit it, and say with Mr. Hall, that baptism was required "to evince the possession of christian sincerity;" we ask then, if this was its design at first, is it not its design *now?* But if so, all the hard things which he has thought fit to say against those who view baptism as the first, visible, appointed evidence of putting on Jesus Christ, he might urge against such as adopt his own words, and plead the importance of the institution for the purpose of evincing "the possession of christian sincerity." If it was once "necessary" for that end, but is not "necessary" for the like purpose at present, what end is answered by it? It is "a duty of perpetual obligation," (*Reply p.* 98.) "founded on the express injunction of the legislator," *(p-* 99,) but, on our author's principles, neither the "duty" nor the "injunction," however "perpetual" or "express," form a rule for the conduct of the church; and though it "*was* necessary" formerly, yet it does not occupy "the same place at present." If such an opinion is admitted, we ought to lay the institution aside; for its original purpose is no longer answered—a consequence which always follows Mr. Hall's theory, on whatever side we view it.

But we have an additional objection to urge. It is not stated in any part of the New Testament, that baptism was an evidence of faith "as it was necessary to evince the possession of christian sincerity." That it *did* "evince christian sincerity" is granted; but that this is the scriptural description of its design, can never be proved. The baptism of the primitive converts was viewed as a practical declaration of their faith; this is manifest from the language of the Apostles: "Ye are all the children of God by faith in Christ Jesus. For as many of you as have been baptised into Christ have *put on Christ*." Gal. iii. 26, 27. Inspired writers treat this subject in a style very different from that of our author. They point the attention of the primitive christians to the great sentiments which they professed to believe at their baptism—to that obligation to holiness which was acknowledged by their baptism—and to the hope which they derived from the truths they had professed, an impressive image of which was presented to their view in baptism. Hence, as many as were baptised into Christ were baptised *into his death.* Faith in the death of Christ, not only as a fact, but as the ground of our justification before God, was the source of their hope, and the great support of their christian life : hence also, believers looked forward to all the blessings which are procured by the resurrection of their Lord. "Therefore," says the apostle, "we are buried with him by baptism into death, that like as Christ was raised from the dead by the glory of the Father, even so we also should walk in newness of life."—"We have been planted together," intimately united with him, "in the likeness of his death," and hence, "we shall be also in the likeness of his resurrection." *Rom.* vi. 3, &c. So also in the epistle to the Colossians, (*chap.* ii. 12.) "Buried with him in baptism, *wherein* also ye are risen with him, through the faith of the operation of God, who hath raised him from the dead." Now, however the latter expression is understood, it is manifest, that it was in consequence of a christian's *faith*, and as an expression of his *faith*, that he was buried with his Lord, when he was baptised in his name.

The Apostle Peter's words are, if possible, still more express. 1 *Pet.* iii. 21. Baptism is "the answer of a good conscience towards God, through the resurrection of Jesus Christ." It is the "answer," the promise, or the stipulation of a good conscience, in consequence of faith in the resurrection of Jesus Christ. It is the expression of a solemn engagement into which we enter, in obedience to a divine command, and as the effect of faith in the Lord Jesus.

If baptism either ought not, or cannot be administered with these views, it is time that we should drop the practice ; but if believers *can*, and *do* express these sentiments, hopes, and engagements, the ordinance in its essential parts, *does* occupy the same place *now*, that it did in the times of the apostles."

Why our author so carefully avoids stating the scriptural design of baptism, is best known to himself, but it is impossible not to suspect that he saw the danger of so doing. He would not say, that baptism ought *not* to be administered on a profession of faith : that would have involved him both with the apostles, and himself. He did not choose to allow, as he had done before, that it ought to be administered on a profession of faith ;—that would be followed by an inference opposite to his purpose. He therefore took a different course, and then he could caricature every thing that came in his way, as he pleased.

Before he finished his second chapter, he made a bold thrust, and doubtless he thought it would be mortal in its effect. He closed one paragraph by speaking of those who are destitute of "*adult* baptism," and professing to quote what we had said, the next begins thus : (*Reply p.* 56.) "No church, he assures us, acting agreeably to the rules of Christ, can recognise them as his disciples." The reference at the bottom is, "*Baptism a term of Communion, p.* 140." If the reader turns to the passage, he will see that *these are* NOT *our words.* But passing this for the present, Mr. Hall takes no notice of the object of that paragraph from which he professes to quote an expression. He does not inform his reader that the point there in hand was, the obligation we were under to attend to baptism as a commanded duty, "*whatever that rite shall prove to be*": for this would have spoiled the effect which he intended to produce. Nor does he at all refer to the evidence adduced in the connection, that the proposition as we had stated and explained it, had been generally admitted not only by *Baptists*, but also by PÆDOBAPTISTS: for they had both agreed that the *unbaptised*, according to the plan of the New Testament, were not openly, and in an acknowledged sense, *disciples.* The general sentiments of those "myriads of holy men," who are sometimes placed in array against us, are brought to view in the words of DR. WILLIAMS and RICHARD BAXTER, both of whom it will be allowed, are high authorities. These eminent men go farther than even the *Baptists* in affirming the proposition which we had laid down, in the sense in which it was adduced. If Mr. Hall *did* perceive the author's design, in the paragraph from which he professes to select a single expression, and especially, if he ever read the succeeding paragraph, how could he, in common justice, bring forward an expression with the intention of impressing on the minds of *his* readers a sentiment not contained in the passage he pretends to quote? If he did *not* perceive the author's intention, how are we to account for such a misconception? But hence an occasion is found for exclaiming, "what strange magic lies concealed in the word *church!*"(*Reply p.* 57.) Again, "in the broad daylight of the world, notwithstanding their minor differences, they (the Pædobaptists) are recognized with facility, but the moment we enter the *sombrous gloom* of a BAPTIST CHURCH, we are lost from each other's view." *(p.* 58.) What advantage Mr. Hall expects from these bitter words, we know not; be it to himself: we ask no participation in it. A reproach so indiscriminate and unjust, may gratify those who dislike the Baptists, but effectually discredits all our author's boasted pretensions to liberality. He talks about inflicting " a wound on the very heart of charity;" (*Reply p.* 87.) what this is we leave others to decide. To such an accusation we reply in the words of an ancient and high authority, " the Lord rebuke thee:" (*Jude v.* 9.) and were the controversy merely with Mr. Hall, here our reply should end. But as a heavy charge is publicly brought forward against a general body, it demands a farther examination. What occasions this "*sombrous gloom* of a BAPTIST *Church*"? Nothing, but their belief that professing christians ought to be baptized, before they are acknowledged members of the church. An article of faith common to all the churches of the apostolic and primitive ages;—to all the established churches in the world;—and, on our author's own confession, nearly to all the churches of Pædobaptist dissenters. "Of such societies," says Mr. Hall, "we might be tempted to exclaim, 'My soul come not thou into their secret, and to their assembly be not thou united"! Here we ask, to what "assembly", then, should we be "united"? The only reply that we can conceive is, to that which admits the *unbaptised:* an assembly evidently of recent date, notwithstanding all that Mr. Hall can say to the contrary; and, on his own acknowledgment, an assembly formed of the minority of christian professors. In all the rest we are compelled to enter the same "sombrous gloom", which Mr. Hall asserts is thrown exclusively over BAPTIST CHURCHES! It is, therefore, very little to the purpose, that he professes to be "shocked at such illiberality;" and still less that he pretends to "suppress the emotions which naturally arise on the occasion, remembering (strange as it may seem) how often it is associated with talents the most respectable, and piety the most fervent". (*Reply p.* 59.) The wound which he intended to inflict can never be healed by such treatment as this.

CHAPTER IV.

AN EXAMINATION OF MR. HALL'S THIRD CHAPTER ON THE CONNECTION BETWEEN THE TWO POSITIVE INSTITUTES.

SECTION I.

His statement of the question examined;—his reasoning refuted.

IN the progress of his work, our author frequently directs the reader's attention to what he calls the "real question," (*p.* 61.) which, he informs us, is, "whether the two positive ordinances of the New Testament are *so related to* each other, either in the nature of things or by express command, that he whom we deem not baptised, is, *ipso facto*, or from that circumstance alone, disqualified for an attendance at the Lord's table. "This," he says, "and this only is the question in which we are concerned."

Two sources of evidence are mentioned, "the nature of things," and, "express command;" no notice is here taken of the *order* and *design* of the institutions; should it be said these are included in the "nature of things," we shall not object to the arrangement; but if they are not included, we contend that they ought to be added to the sources of evidence by which the question is to be decided.

According to *Mr. Hall*, " that there is not a necessary *connection* in the nature of things betwixt the two rites, appears from the slightest attention to their *nature*. It will not be pretended that the Lord's supper is *founded* on baptism, or that it recognises a single circumstance belonging to it." (*Reply p.* 61, 62.)

According to JESUS CHRIST, the order and design of baptism show, that it was intended to precede an attention to every other institution which he commanded the members of his church " to observe ;" and according to the APOSTLE PAUL, baptism is " putting on Christ." *Gal.* iii. 27. The Lord's supper is designed for believers who are members of his church, and *recognises* a previous profession of their faith. What, then, was included in this profession—how was it made—what was the visible appointed rite by which a submission to Jesus Christ was manifested, according to the directions and examples of the New Testament? Let this question be answered and the connection will be established.

But by his own concessions, Mr. Hall has already answered the question and established the connection. He has allowed that " baptism OUGHT, *agreeably to the institution of Christ*, to precede the other branches of religion;" (*p.* 83.) and that " supposing [the sincere believer] to be clearly convinced of the *nature* and *import* of baptism, he would be guilty of a *criminal irregularity* who neglected to attend to it *previous* to his entering into christian fellowship." (*Terms of Com. p.* 58.) In the view of this sincere believer, there is consequently a " necessary connection" between the two ordinances, which he perceives when he is " clearly convinced of the *nature* and *import* of baptism ;" otherwise he could not be guilty of a " *criminal irregularity*" in seeking communion without being baptised. On what principle then, can it be maintained that there *is* such a " connection" when the " nature and import" of baptism is understood, but no " connection" between the institutions themselves? Does not the connection exist before it is perceived? Is it, or is it not correct that baptism has a "prior claim" on the christian's attention? Such priority, however, Mr. Hall has distinctly acknowledged, for he admits that " baptism OUGHT, *agreeably to the institution of Christ to* PRECEDE the other branches of religion." Thus he confesses that which he is trying to prove does not exist; and all his arguments to shew that there is no connection between the two institutions, are repelled by his own words.

He then says, "it remains to be considered whether the *necessary connection* we are seeking, can be found in positive prescription.—Here, when we ask for bread, they give us a stone," *(p. 63.)* Perhaps so; there is a "prescription" so "positive" in the terms of the commission of our Lord, that it is "a stone" of stumbling to our author's system which cannot be removed. Let the reader observe his statement, "They quote Christ's commission to his apostles, where there is not a word upon the subject, and which is so remote from establishing the essential *connection* of the two ceremonies, that the mention of one of them only is included."(*p.*63.) "Remote" as the commission is, according to Mr. Hall's account, we have only to follow its directions, and there will be an end of his system. "Of the two ceremonies—the *mention* of one of them only is included." It is allowed that *one is mentioned*; the most unfortunate circumstance possible for our author's argument; for, as the "*only*" ceremony which our Lord thought it necessary to "mention" was baptism, the "mention" of that "one" institution gave it distinguished prominency. It was, however, *mentioned* in the style of authority; the Saviour enjoined his apostles to baptise those that believed, and he then directed them to teach those who believed and were baptised, "*to observe*" all things whatsoever he had commanded them. *Matt.* xxviii. 19, 20. Let Mr. Hall therefore either acknowledge, or deny, that the Lord's supper was one of those things which the disciples were commanded "*to observe.*" If he acknowledges it, the "connection" is sufficiently established for all practical purposes. If he denies it, we shall calmly wait for the proof of so extraordinary a position. If that "one" institution, which it is granted our Lord *did* "mention", *is* obeyed, neither party will doubt the propriety of admitting any person applying for communion, if in other respects he is eligible; if it is acknowledged that it *ought to be* obeyed, there is no occasion for us to deliver an opinion, for Mr. Hall tells us that baptism has a "prior claim" to attention.

He adds, "they urge the conduct of the apostles, though it is not only sufficiently accounted for on our principles, but it is such as those *very principles* would in their circumstances have absolutely compelled us to adopt." (*p.* 63.) This argument has occurred before, and we have already replied to it; at present, therefore, we shall only observe, that if in the apostles' days Mr. Hall must have refused the unbaptised, but *now* ought to receive them, the authority and permanency of baptism is gone. For if it is not the will of Christ that his church should support an institution of his appointment, in its primitive station, the inevitable inference is, that it was either *temporary*, or so connected with the peculiar circumstances of the primitive times, that afterwards it became of no practical consequence.

Again, "They [the apostles] baptised, because they were commanded to do so; they administered the Lord's supper, because our Saviour enjoined it on his disciples; and both these duties were prescribed to the societies they formed, *because the nature and obligation of each were equally and perfectly understood.*" (*p.* 64.) Now, without inquiring whether the reason why "both these duties were prescribed" is, or is not correct, it is manifest, that when the "nature and obligation of each [of these duties] were *equally and perfectly understood,"* the Lord's supper was *never* administered to the *unbaptised,* on Mr. Hall's own confession. But how could a perfect understanding of their *" nature,"* place them in such an order, if there was not some reason why that order ought to be followed?

The stress which he lays on the "nature and obligation" of these injunctions being " equally and perfectly understood," will avail him nothing. For when we have to discuss the subject with a person who denies the perpetuity of baptism, our object is to prove that it was the design of the Lord that it should be continued in his church; but whenever the perpetuity of both ordinances is acknowledged, their " nature" is sufficiently understood to settle the present controversy; for who will affirm, that according to the New Testament, baptism was not designed to *precede* the Lord's supper? Even on Mr. Hall's principles, should any one come forward and say, he admitted the perpetuity of these institutions, but though unbaptised, yet he requested communion, such an application ought to be rejected.

Still it may be said, there is no "necessary connection", no " immutable relation" between the two ordinances. Here we would ask, what is meant by the terms? Positive precepts depend on the will of the legislator; if that is expressed with sufficient clearness, so that according to the "natural order of the christian sacraments," baptism has the "prior claim"; there is enough to guide the mind of the man who with simplicity of heart inquires what is the will of Christ, and to form in his view a "connection" so "necessary", a "relation" so "immutable", that he dares not break it.

The only remaining supposition is, that though there may be some connection between the two institutions, yet they are not " *so* related to each other"—that he whom we deem not baptised, is, *ipso facto,* or from that circumstance alone, disqualified for an attendance at the Lord's table". (*p. 61.*) We then inevitably come to this conclusion—the revealed will of Christ is, that both the ordinances ought to be obeyed in the order in which they are laid down, but conformity to what is confessed to be his will is not necessary! A proposition which, if proved, would we grant, settle the controversy; but it would be, by disannulling the authority of the rule of our conduct; and would dissolve all obligation to make the New Testament our guide, either in the formation or constitution of the christian church.

We therefore take the consequence which is pressed upon us. " He whom we deem unbaptised is, from that circumstance alone, disqualified for an attendance at the Lord's table", with those who deem him unbaptised. For they cannot admit him, without acknowledging, that baptism is now become a matter of great indifference; and that whatever have been its claims, they have so far vanished, that the original importance of the institution is gone, its authority is virtually repealed; and what was once a leading article in the constitution of the christian church, is no more of any consequence. But, " in the present case it is sufficient for us to know, that whatever God has thought fit to enjoin, must be a matter of duty; and it little becomes weak and finite mortals to limit its sphere, or explain away its obligation, by refined and subtle distinctions". *(p. 63.)*

We are also informed, that "it surely requires but little attention to perceive that it is one thing to *tolerate,* and another to *sanction*; that to affirm that each of the positive rites of religion ought to be attended to; and that they are so *related,* that a mistake respecting one, instantly disqualifies for another, are not the same propositions". *(p. 61.)* " An attention to this distinction," we are told " would have incredibly shortened the present debate." We have no objection to view the subject in any light which will at once enable us to see its proper issue. We shall have occasion in our progress to notice at large our author's reasoning respecting "toleration"; for the present we shall only ask, if we " *tolerate*" the admission of those who are acknowledged to be unbaptised, do we not " sanction" their communion *in that character?* The question thus practically comes to a single point—can Mr. Hall prove that we act according to the New Testament rule and examples, in forming a church of *unbaptised* members? We say to him as we say to the Pædobaptists, produce a *single instance* from the word of God in proof of your theory, and we will be silent.

It has been said by some persons, that, "as the apostolic commission was only the law of baptism, nothing respecting a *subsequent institution* can be inferred from it."* But the commission itself asserts the contrary. It directed the Apostles to teach the baptised, "to observe all things whatsoever" the Lord "commanded" them; thus it was not, "only the law of baptism", it was more; it was a law enjoining those who by baptism had " put on Christ," to obey all his commands. Whether that ordinance, here called " a *subsequent institution*," was among the number, we leave the common sense of men to determine. But if the apostolic commission continues as a rule, the only question which, in any instance, we have to settle is, whether " the law of baptism," has been obeyed, or not? for the Lord's supper is " a SUBSEQUENT *institution*," even on the concession of our opponents.

* Congregational Mag. June 1818. p. 324.

SECTION II.

Mistakes of Mr. Hall respecting Mr. Fuller—the Unities, Eph. iv.—and, Dr. Whitby.

In " Baptism a term of communion" an argument is adduced, which was borrowed from "Mr. Fuller's Letter to a Friend," intitled "The admission of unbaptised persons to the Lord's supper, inconsistent with the New Testament." We stated the substance of one of Mr. Fuller's arguments, though we did not copy his words. Mr. Hall quotes our words, as if they were Mr. Fuller's: we then added some observations on the *Unities* mentioned Eph. iv. 3, &c. These he also considers as Mr. Fuller's, though they are *not his*, nor is there any thing in the connection that would lead an attentive reader to this conclusion. We then find a critique on Mr. Fuller's pamphlet, in which he speaks of it in a very degrading manner, and reflects on the editor for publishing it.

It was not unnatural for Mr. Hall to think lightly of Mr. Fuller's work on a point opposed to his own favourite theory: but why he should say, Mr. F— " felt some distrust of the ground he was treading, *which for several reasons* I strongly suspect," we know not. In conversations which the writer of these pages had with him on the subject some months before his death, he appeared satisfied that his views were correct: and this is strongly attested by the advertisement which is prefixed to the pamphlet. In that advertisement there is an extract of a letter sent with the manuscript to Dr. Newman, dated Jan. 16, 1815, in which Mr. Fuller says, "if any thing be written on the other side, it may, if thought proper, be printed, but not else." Mr. Fuller died before Mr. Hall's treatise on " Terms of Communion" was published : when that work appeared, Dr. Newman justly thought that he ought no longer to withhold Mr. Fuller's letter.

Those who read only what Mr. Hall has said concerning it, will suppose that Mr. Fuller's work contains nothing more than the arguments he has noticed. But they who read the work for themselves, will find many things which bear on the point, and which, though they are stated briefly, deserve consideration: and they will then judge of the accuracy which Mr. Hall displayed, when he brought together, an argument which we borrowed from Mr. Fuller,—some observations of our own for which he is not accountable,—and then added—" such is the substance of Mr. Fuller's *argumentation* on this subject"! *(p.* 68.)

But to return : Mr. Fuller's argument was drawn from passages he had quoted, in which allusions were made to baptism and the Lord's supper in a manner which shewed the two ordinances were connected together in the mind of the Apostle. (*Fuller's Letter, p.* 17—19. *Baptism a term of Com. p.* 27, 28.) In his " Reply," p. 65, Mr. Hall says, " It is freely admitted that these, and perhaps other texts which might be adduced, afford examples of an allusion to the two ordinances at the same time, whence we may be certain that they were *present together in the mind of the writer*. But whoever considers the laws of association, must be aware how trivial a circumstance is sufficient to unite together in the mind, ideas of objects among which no essential relation exists." Again, " In fact the warmest advocates of *our* practice would feel no sort of difficulty in adopting the same style, in an epistle to a church which consisted *only of baptists:* consequently nothing more can be inferred than that *the societies which St. Paul addressed were universally of that description :* a fact we have already fully conceded. The only light in which it bears on the subject is that which makes it perfectly coincide with the argument from primitive precedent, the futility of which has been sufficiently demonstrated." *(p.* 65, 66.)

Here let us observe what our author has conceded. It is allowed that the societies whom *Paul* addressed were *universally* BAPTISTS, and that in his address, the two ordinances *were present together* in his mind: nay farther, that Mr. H. and the advocates of his practice, would feel no sort of difficulty in addressing "a church which consisted *only of Baptists*" in the same style. So that it is only in a *Baptist church* the expressions of the Apostle can be used with propriety, Mr. Hall himself being judge!

As an apology for the Apostles' alluding to the two ordinances at the same time, we are told that "whoever considers the laws of association, must be aware how *trivial* a circumstance is sufficient to unite together in the mind, ideas of objects among which no essential relation subsists." We are told, that "the mere coincidence of time and place is abundantly sufficient for that purpose." The force of this reasoning is, that because a vagrant imagination will connect things which have no relation, but which are united by a *"trivial circumstance,"* therefore, so might the Apostle; and for this reason we should not suppose that there was any "essential relation" subsisting between the two ordinances, though we are certain that "they were present together" in his mind.

But it is not enough to assert, that a "trivial circumstance" is sufficient to unite together in the mind the ideas of objects not related to each other; it should be *proved* that in the present instance it was *only* a "trivial circumstance" that *did* associate the two ordinances in the view of the Apostle. It should be *proved* that notwithstanding the prominency given to baptism in the commission, and in the practice of the christian church—notwithstanding, on our author's own confession, it was *then* essential, not only to communion but to salvation, yet it was connected with the Lord's supper in the Apostle's mind by so slight a bond, that it is by this time completely broken. But be the connection what it may, baptism appears the *first* in the order here before us; and how can it be accounted for, that both the facts and allusions place it thus, unless it was commanded to be administered *first*. So that whatever is the weight of this argument, it lies entirely on *one side*; and wherever a church is formed on Mr. Hall's principles, the apostolic style of address must be discontinued.

The next attack is made on the "*Unities*," enumerated in Eph. iv. 4, 5, 6; particularly the "one baptism", ver. 5. Mr. Hall calls this text "irrelevant to the present argument." (*p.* 66.) His reasons are, "since no mention is made of the Lord's supper, it cannot be intended to confirm, or illustrate, the relation which baptism bears to that ordinance." The Apostle was speaking of the unities by which the church was distinguished—and one of these was baptism. But, according to the description before us, how could a person become a member of the church who was not baptised? and how could he who was not a member be admitted to the Lord's supper? Besides, if there is any force in Mr. Hall's reasoning, it is against himself: for, "since no mention is made of the Lord's supper," it is not included among the unities necessary to be found in the christian church; but baptism, from the distinct mention made of it, *is* necessary. A christian society may bear all the marks here given of a christian church, though it may for a time be deprived of the Lord's supper; but it does not answer the description of the Apostle if it has not baptism.

Again, "it is very uncertain [says Mr. Hall] whether the Apostle refers to water baptism, or to the baptism of the spirit; but admitting that he intends the *latter*, [perhaps a misprint for the *former*] he asserts no more than we firmly believe, that there are not two or more valid baptisms under the christian dispensation, but *one* only;

a deviation from which, either with respect to the *subject,* or the *mode, reduces it to a nullity.*" (*p.* 66, 67.) Here it is conceded that there is *one*—only *one* valid baptism: and virtually, that *Pædobaptism* is a *nullity.*

He adds, "Lastly, since his [the Apostle's] avowed object in insisting upon these *unities,* was to persuade his reader to maintain inviolate that unity of spirit to which they *were all subservient,* it is extremely unreasonable to adduce this passage in defence of a practice which involves its subversion." (*p.* 67.) So then, the effect which the Apostle had in view, and to which *all* the enumerated unities *were subservient,* will be better produced by leaving one of them out! Pleading for one of these *unities,* and we hope, not improperly pleading for that unity both of faith and of spirit with the primitive church, which arises from making it our model both as to sentiment and practice, is subverting that unity!

But the system of the Apostle and that of our author are widely different. Paul expressly mentions baptism and omits the Lord's supper. Mr. Hall excludes baptism as unnecessary to unity, and would have us turn our attention peculiarly to the latter institute. The Apostle says distinctly, the primitive church had "ONE *baptism*"; our author, it is true, allows that there are not "two or more valid baptisms, but *one* only"; yet the whole of his labour is to bring in those who, on his own acknowledgment, have had NO *baptism!* The two theories are so far asunder, that it is impossible to adopt both.

To close the whole, the authority of a "learned commentator,"—"the celebrated WHITBY, a Pædobaptist, and an Episcopalian," is brought against us; and a passage is quoted with great approbation; the principal part of which is, "that no error in judgment, or mistake in practice, which doth not tend to deprive a christian of the spirit of Christ, can separate him from the church of Christ." "Thus it is, that this learned commentator conceives himself to have discovered a demonstration of the principles we are abetting, in the very words our opponents urge for their overthrow." *(p.* 67, 68.)

It is no part of our intention to undervalue *Dr. Whitby*. Though many of the Baptists do not on certain points agree with this "learned commentator," yet he shall have full credit for all his excellencies. Let us, however, hear his own statement. In the paraphrase which he gives of the chapter previous to the Annotations, he says, on verse the 5th, "There is also to us christians one Lord, one faith in this Lord, one baptism *by which we do profess this faith.*" *Dr. Whitby's* evident design in the Annotations from which Mr. Hall has copied the "demonstration" of *his* principles, is to oppose the arguments of the Catholics, and to prove that "no church governors, jointly or severally, can be by God appointed to be the living judges, or the infallible directors of our faith." But in urging this conclusion, did he intend to deny his own *Paraphrase?* If not, how did christians come into the church? Dr. Whitby tells us—there is "one faith in this Lord, and one baptism *by which we do profess this faith.*" In this instance Dr. W. pleads the cause which *we* advocate; and his inferences are denied by no protestant of any party. Our controversy is not, on what grounds a person should be separated from the church of Christ, who has become a member of that body according to the New Testament plan, but on what grounds he ought to be *admitted*.

SECTION III.

Mr. Hall's reasoning concerning positive law and prohibition, examined.

MR. HALL next professes to inquire whether the two institutions of the Gospel " are connected by *positive* law. Is there a single word in the New Testament which, fairly interpreted, can be regarded as a *prohibition* of the admission of unbaptised persons to the Lord's supper?" (*p.* 69.) Here Mr. Hall attempts to take advantage of an expression in 'Baptism a Term of Communion,' p. 32, which is, "the New Testament does not prohibit the unbaptised from receiving the Lord's supper, because no circumstance arose which rendered such prohibition necessary." We stated three things; Mr. Hall chooses to omit one, and blend the other two together. If the reader will refer to the above-mentioned treatise, he will find that the sentence quoted by Mr. Hall, was preceded by this observation, "surely it will not be pleaded, that a command is *not binding*, except there be a prohibition of its opposite. If a direction be plainly delivered, and those who hear it conceive that they clearly understand it, that ought to be enough." Here an appeal is made to *positive law ;* and a prohibition was stated not to be necessary, whenever the sense of that positive law was clearly perceived. For however men may differ in their interpretation of the command which enjoins baptism, there is not a pretence for saying, that those who admit its authority and perpetuity, need such a prohibition. Who that allows the permanency of the institution, will say, it ought not to be obeyed ?—and if it ought to be obeyed, who will venture to assert, that it should be placed *after* communion.

Mr. Hall thinks proper to say, that the only reason assigned "for an express prohibition not being then necessary, is, that the ordinance of baptism was perfectly understood:" and he then adds, "surely if this be the *only* reason, the necessity must return when that reason ceases; or in other words, there will be a necessity for an express prohibition of the unbaptised whenever the precept respecting baptism ceases to be understood." (*p.* 71.)

If the reader will attend to a few plain observations, he will easily be able to judge of Mr. Hall's correctness in examining a statement, or in reasoning upon it. *He* says the ONLY reason which we assigned why a prohibition was not necessary, was that the ordinance was perfectly understood. If any person will examine what we *did* say, he will find;—1st. It was supposed, that a prohibition would not be deemed necessary to give force to a clear command. 2dly. It was observed, "That the New Testament does not prohibit the unbaptised from receiving the Lord's supper, *because no circumstance arose which rendered such prohibition necessary.*" It does not appear that any of the principles on which the moderns have advocated the cause of mixed communion had been heard of. There was no need to *prohibit* what no one thought of doing. Had there been a tendency to our author's mode of reasoning in the minds of any member of the primitive church, the subject might have excited attention. It might have been said, extreme cases sometimes occur; is there no reservation made in their favour? But either none of this kind occurred, or if they did occur, we have no evidence that the rule was dispensed with on their account. It was then added, 3dly. "It is *acknowledged,* that the law of baptism was clearly understood, and that the unbaptised could not be received into the church. There was therefore no reason why a prohibitory declaration should exist." (*Baptism a term of Com. p.* 32.) Here let it be remarked, our observation was founded on what *Mr. Hall* had *acknowledged*. *He* therefore could not, with any share of reason, demand a prohibition of what he himself confessed could not exist.

Leaving the reader to judge how far our author is correct in his statement, let us follow him in his argument, " if this be the *only* reason, the necessity must return when that reason ceases;" &c. (*p.* 71.) Whether it was the *only* reason can easily be determined; but if no other had been assigned, the inspired writers did not anticipate arguments which, in future ages, might be urged against what was understood and practised in their time. They deemed it quite sufficient to shew how *they* reasoned, how *they* acted, and to rectify those who in their day were attempting to introduce innovations. Those who in after times choose to act a different part, are left to do as they please. As BISHOP BURNET says, (speaking of the alterations which the Papists made in the Lord's supper) " All reasoning upon this head is an arguing against the institution; as if Christ and his apostles had not well enough considered it; but that twelve hundred years after them, a consequence should be observed that till then had not been thought of, which made it reasonable to alter the manner of it." (*Expos. of the Articles, Art.* 30.) If we are required to bring " an express prohibition of the unbaptised," a Pædobaptist may demand " an express prohibition" of infant baptism; a Churchman, of kneeling at the Lord's supper; and a Roman Catholic, of all the ceremonies of his church. Should it be said, these practices are inconsistent with the obvious intention of many parts of the New Testament, we reply, and so is the admission of the unbaptised.

But, on our author's mode of reasoning, even a "prohibition" might with the greatest ease be set aside. It could not be more plainly *prohibited* that the christian convert should partake of the Lord's supper BEFORE he was baptised, than it is *commanded* that he should be BAPTISED.

Yet if any one should say, that he believed baptism itself was a temporary institution, he might, on our author's principles, be admitted to communion without hesitation. For, however strongly the prohibition was expressed, that the unbaptised should not partake of it, it might still be replied, all this was true *once* while baptism was in force, but *now* the connection between the two ordinances is dissolved, and the prohibition abrogated. If, then, he who denies the authority of baptism altogether may be received, he who denies the force of a prohibition (which could not last longer than the ordinance to which it related) should not be rejected. What, then, would either the directions or the prohibitions of Scripture avail, when maxims which lead to such results are set in high places?

Doubtless Mr. Hall expects to confound us by his succeeding argument. "Has it, [the precept respecting baptism] or has it not, ceased (in our apprehension) to be understood by modern Pædobaptists? If it be admitted that it has, then, on his own principle, an express *prohibition of the unbaptised* to receive the Lord's supper has become necessary." (*p.* **71.**) A powerful appeal indeed! —but to use the words of *Bishop Taylor*, " it is a goodly harangue, which upon strict examination will come to nothing—it pretends fairly and signifies little."*

It is right to separate what *has*, from what has *not ceased* to be *understood*. Mr. Hall endeavours to perplex the argument by drawing off his reader's attention from the important consequences arising from this distinction. We retort therefore his own reasoning:—" Has it, or has it not, ceased to be understood by modern Pædobaptists," that according to the New Testament, baptism ought to precede the Lord's supper? On this point we have had as yet, no controversy with them, nor do we expect any. For unless they were to introduce *infant communion*, and were to give the Lord's supper *before* they administered

---

* Liberty of Prophesying, § 18. p. **228.** Ed. 1647—4to.

baptism, their conduct shews that they and we understand this part of the subject alike. So that if there were a "prohibition" in terms ever so "express", they would reply, this does not affect *us*; for we believe that we *are* baptised.—Should they, however, profess an alteration in their sentiments, and declare that the baptised and the unbaptised have an *equal right* to communion, we will consider their arguments as soon as we hear them. Till then, Mr. Hall's question, bold as it is, does not require an answer.

SECTION IV.

Mr. Hall's evasion of the argument on the connection of the two ordinances—his accusations confronted—his mistakes concerning the "Scottish Baptists", &c.

WE now come to Mr. Hall's attack on a few expressions in 'Baptism a term of Communion,' on the connection between baptism and the Lord's supper. The first passage is taken from p. 30—"if the above evidence be justly stated, there is a real instituted connection between baptism and the whole succeeding christian profession. So that there is no reason why the connection between baptism and the Lord's supper should be more distinctly marked than between baptism and any other duty or privilege." In this passage the connection pleaded for, is stated as an inference from evidence which had been adduced: the appeal (as we have before stated) had been made to the New Testament: to the *principle* which runs through the whole body of fact recorded in the apostolic writings; and to those collateral evidences which arose from the notice taken of the ordinances of the gospel in the Epistles of Paul. Baptism was a visible, ritual observance; it was commanded by the Lord, and had its appointed place. Among the various duties which marked the visible profession of christianity, baptism took the lead. It laid the christian under an obligation to "*observe*" all that the Lord had commanded: it was the first link in the chain, and the rest followed in their order.

Here Mr. Hall flies from the subject. He seems aware that the New Testament says nothing that favours communion with persons unbaptised, and that it is in vain to go to that volume for proof of what was unknown till centuries after it was written. No objection is therefore made to the evidence produced; but he attempts to overset the whole by an inference:—" if this be the case, why do they confine their restriction to the mere act of communion at the Lord's table? In every other respect they feel no scruple in acknowledging the members of other denominations as *christians*," &c. (*p.* 73.) The whole of Mr. Hall's attack proceeds on the assumption, that we ought not to consider those as christians with whom we do not think it right to commune: an opinion which protestants justly treat as an absurdity, and which flourishes no where in so much vigour as in the church of Rome. We might refer to preceding observations, which shew that we did not place the argument on a ground that unchristianised those who differ with us; we adopted a theory so different from that imputed to us, that if the reader peruses the two pages of "Baptism a term of Communion", which lie open when he refers to one of Mr. Hall's quotations on this subject, he will usually find that his representations are in some material part flatly contradicted. But it is not worth following him in his misrepresentations. He may, as long as he pleases, stigmatise those who do not think as he does; this may seriously injure *him*, but it cannot hurt *them*. He may exclaim—" what in the mean time becomes of apostolic practice and ancient precedent? How admirably are these illustrated by their judicious selection of the Lord's table, as the spot on which to suspend the ensigns of party." (*p.* 75)—and doubtless many people think this is an admirable stroke ! But may not the same thing be said in every instance in which any body of christians, taking the New Testament for their guide, have left a church which they thought had departed from the primitive standard, and formed one which they deemed more agreeable to the will of Christ? The same imputation falls on every protestant community in the world ; for whatever produces a separation of communion for the purpose of fulfilling the will of Christ, may always have such harsh terms applied to it.

Mr. Hall is at full liberty to brand us as a " party"; but if we are a similar " party" to that body of christians which existed in the days of inspiration ; if like them we walk in the " Apostle's doctrine and in fellowship ;" if like them we have " one Lord, one faith, one baptism," we are contented ; and we accept the censure which he, or any man casts upon us, as the consequence of our holding fast " the faith once delivered to the Saints." It is nothing more than a repetition of the Jewish reproach, " as concerning this sect, we know that every where it is spoken against."

Ever since the commencement of the Reformation the question has often been discussed, how far ought christians to conform to the platform laid down in the New Testament, in the structure and regulation of the church? That portion of the inquiry now in hand, contains only a small part of the general question, and lies in a narrow compass. Jesus Christ left *only two* visible institutions in his church, and the present discussion practically leads us to ask, shall we support the authority of *one* of them, or shall we neglect it? If we ought to dismantle the church of one of its ordinances—if it is of little consequence whether it is obeyed correctly, or incorrectly, or even denied altogether—if a plan confessedly opposite to the constant practice of apostolic times ought to be adopted, and that which visibly appears on the face of the New Testament ought to be violently opposed as *unchristian*, then we acknowledge we are wrong. But unless these particulars are proved against us from a clear and sound interpretation of the New Testament, we need not be solicitous about our defence.

"Apostolic practice and ancient precedent" are not easily set aside. Expressions of ours Mr. Hall can torture and pervert; the body with which he is connected he can degrade, and treat with great contempt; but the undeniable practice of the inspired servants of the Lord still remains, and will remain, as a stumbling block in his way. And while he is compelled to confess that the baptists are the only body of christians that are baptised, the ground which we occupy is instantly seen to be strong, if the New Testament is to be our guide in the formation of the church.

The provocation which he feels is increased by our continuing not to condemn those as destitute of christianity, who in our opinion are not correct in their judgment and practice on the point of baptism. Hence violent efforts are made to accuse us of inconsistency. A portion of this irritation of spirit was to be expected from the too common effect of controversy; but when both the expressions and argument of an opponent are distorted, and turned to purposes which were never designed, it is then evident, that there is some unmanageable impediment which cannot be removed;—some argument adduced, which if not noisy, is distinct and forcible, and which is attempted to be run down because it cannot be answered.

A passage occurs in Mr. Hall's "Reply," (*p.* 75,) which clearly marks the state of his mind on the present subject. He says, "when we read of Priscilla and Aquila taking Apollos home, and instructing him in the way of the Lord more perfectly, *we give full credit to the narrative;* but had we been informed that these excellent persons, after hearing him with great delight, refused his admission to the supper of the Lord, on account of some diversity of opinion, or of practice, the consent of all the manuscripts and versions in the world would have been insufficient to overcome the *incredulity* arising from an instantaneous conviction of its *total repugnance* to the maxims and principles of primitive christianity. Yet this would have been nothing more than an anticipation of the practice of our opponents." Bring the case to its proper point; suppose that Apollos, who knew "only the baptism of John," (*Acts* xviii. 25.) was in the same circumstances with the disciples at Ephesus, who were also baptised "unto John's baptism" (*Acts* xix. 3.)—would Priscilla and Aquila have received him to the Lord's supper? If they would not, we see how their conduct would be condemned by Mr. Hall; if they would, how can he account for the conduct of Paul to the Ephesian disciples? He believes that the Apostle commanded them to be "baptised in the name of the Lord Jesus"; but does he believe, or can he prove, that he received these disciples to the Lord's supper *before* they were baptised? On his *own interpretation* of the passage, the conduct of the Apostle in commanding those "to be baptised in the name of the Lord Jesus," whose baptism he considered as imperfect and invalid, was " nothing more than an anticipation" of that practice, which, had it existed in the case before mentioned, Mr. Hall says, would have been in "total repugnance to the maxims and principles of primitive christianity"!

He deserves, however, our thanks for his frankness;

he fairly tells us, that if Priscilla and Aquila had practised strict communion, (which is nothing more than not uniting in church membership with persons acknowledged to be unbaptised) *the consent of all the manuscripts and versions in the world,* would have no weight with *him :* it is a settled point in his mind, that such conduct is repugnant " to the maxims and principles of *primitive* christianity"; and had it been practised by the most "excellent persons" in the times of inspiration, he would not have believed it to be agreeable to the will of Christ!

Besides all that has been urged against us of a nature to which the preceding observations will apply, a new charge is brought forward—" a deviation from ancient precedent"!(*p.* 78.) What is this "deviation?" It is, "that the first christians did not interchange religious services with those with whom they refused to communicate"! A curious accusation indeed. Mr. H. allows that all the primitive churches were baptised; he will not deny that they had " one Lord, one faith, one baptism":—and the time was not arrived when any one imagined the two christian ordinances were independent of each other. That " deviation" from the one baptism of the christian dispensation, " which, either with respect to the subject or the mode, *reduces it to a nullity,*" according to his own acknowledgment had not taken place. So that the question had not occurred, *how far* we might act with those who had made such a "deviation." It is therefore in vain to charge us with departing from " ancient precedent", till our author has produced a precedent which applies to the present case. There are, however, some cases on record which, as far as they resemble the present state of things, deserve consideration, since they furnish us with analogies. The conduct of Paul in directing the Ephesian disciples to be baptised, has been noticed, both in this work, and in ' Baptism a term of Communion ;' and no one will venture to say *this* is an " ancient precedent" against us. The

Apostle thought differently of these disciples than he did of men in general, yet he commanded them to be baptised. So also Priscilla and Aquila did not treat Apollos as a schismatic, but as a mistaken good man. The conduct of the Apostles in attending the temple worship, furnishes another case in our favour. " Peter and John went up together into the temple at the hour of prayer, being the ninth hour." (*Acts* iii. 1.) They did not forsake the house of prayer whither they had been habituated to go, so long as they had the opportunity. The Apostle Paul also, many years afterwards, went up to Jerusalem to *worship:* (*Acts* xxiv. 11.) This is his defence for being found in the temple: and he contended, that though in the way which the Jews call heresy, yet said he, " *so worship I the God of my fathers;*" ver. 14. the same God whom they worshipped; thus declaring that though he differed from them, yet since there was one great point of union, he acceded to their worship as far as he could: and his taking the vow of a Nazarite upon him, and being found in the temple for the purpose of fulfilling the commanded rites, part of which consisted in an offering made by the Jewish Priests according to the law, was a proof that, as far as he thought them right, he gave them such complete countenance, that he made use of their ministrations. Indeed this part of his conduct was designed as a public testimony that he could, and did worship God according to the rites of the Jews; and yet we know that his sentiments as a christian would necessarily prevent him from holding complete communion with that people. So far, therefore, as cases existed which have any resemblance to our having a partial connection with those with whom we cannot altogether agree, the spirit of " ancient precedent" is *not* against us but *for* us. Our maxim is, unite where you can; differ, only when you are compelled by your views of the New Testament pattern of a christian church: and when a better maxim than this is discovered, and proved to be consistent with the sacred volume, we will gladly adopt it.

A curious specimen of quotation occurs in that part of Mr. Hall's work now under examination, and as he seems to think he gains an advantage from what he brings forward, and recurs afterwards to the same thing, it may be proper to notice it in detail. He says, (p. 78.) "Mr. Kinghorn himself deprecates the *very suspicion of placing even baptism on a level with the least of the moral precepts of Christ*." Again, (p. 105)—"Our author acknowledges that baptism is not to be 'compared in importance with the least of Christ's moral precepts'." (p. 107)—"he tells us that he is far from 'equalizing baptism with the least of Christ's moral precepts'." (p. 108)— "the omission of a moral precept—*the least of which*, he affirms, *is of greater moment than baptism.*"

In none of the above pretended quotations does Mr. Hall refer to any page, where such expressions may be found: in two of them he puts certain words with inverted commas, as if these were the very words which we had used. The reader will observe that they are *not* the *same words*; but this would probably lead him to suppose, that the sentiment was repeated with some variation of expression.

The question however returns, where did Mr. Hall find *any* of the professed quotations which he has brought forward?—The answer is—*not* in '*Baptism a term of Communion.*' It is there acknowledged, "that many other things are of greater consequence than baptism" (p. 164.) It is there also said, (p. 87) (which is probably the passage Mr. Hall had in his view)—"these remarks," [referring to preceding observations] "are not made for the purpose of *raising* this institution to an *undue height*; nor in any respect designed to *exalt it in the place of* the Saviour, *or* of faith in him, *or* of *obedience to the least of his moral precepts;* but as they lie on the surface of the New Testament, and have a strong bearing on the present subject, we ought not to pass them without notice."

Here let the reader compare Mr. Hall's professed quotations with our proposition; and let him observe both how different are *the words* which he has put with inverted commas, from those which are copied from the work itself; and how different is their *design*. We plead for the regard due to the first positive christian institute, in the station in which the Lord appointed it, whatever that station is; but we have no wish to *displace* the least of the moral precepts, and make baptism a substitute in its stead. But supposing that Mr. Hall's interpretation had been just, and that the ordinance in question was allowed to be less than any of the moral precepts, and even *the least* of the precepts which Christ commanded, still it is no part of our ambition to "break one of these least commandments and *teach men so*," lest we should be called " *the least* in the kingdom of heaven." *Matt*. v. 19.

A train of confident assertions is brought forward by Mr. Hall, (*p*. 80,) in which we are told, that the advocates of the restrictive system must change their ground; they *must* either go forwards or backwards.—" They have most *unreasonably* and *capriciously* stopped where no mortal before ever thought of staying for a moment!" It is not true that we have "stopped"—" where no mortal before ever thought of staying for a moment". The ground on which we have fixed our " encampment," is easily described;—we maintain the priority of baptism to the Lord's supper, according to the New Testament directions and examples. This is the place at which we have "stopped"; and all who are acquainted with Ecclesiastical History know, that for many centuries after the primitive age, "*no mortal*" ever thought of quitting this ground. We acknowledge that we think better of those who differ from us, than has sometimes been the case with contending parties in past days;—a great crime indeed! If in this part of our conduct we avoid any portion of the mistakes which excellent men made in former times, we assume no merit to ourselves; but we are thankful that we have been led in any measure into a better way.

Mr. Hall thinks proper to call our conduct *unreasonable* and *capricious*. If it is unreasonable, because we will not walk even with good men in a path which we conceive is different from that pointed out by the Legislator of the church, our reply is brief, "whether it be right in the sight of God to hearken unto you, more than unto God, judge ye." (*Acts* iv. 19.) If it be capricious to lay down the plain directions of the New Testament as our rule, and to draw the outline of our "encampment," with that volume in our hand, we had better be reproached for such capriciousness, than for the want of it.

Our author reiterates his stroke; "they have already made such near approaches to the great body of those whom we deem unbaptised, as places them at an immeasurable distance from the *letter* of the apostolic precedent, though in perfect harmony with its spirit; while they preposterously cling to that letter as the reason for refusing to go an inch farther." (*p.* 80.)

Here we ask, what is meant by an "*immeasurable distance* from the letter of apostolic precedent"? Does the "*letter*" of the "apostolic precedent" afford a single instance of membership and communion with the *unbaptised?* If it does, let Mr. Hall produce it. In apostolic example we have NO *precedent* that will justify *uninspired* men in displacing one of the ordinances of the Gospel from its primitive station; but we *have* precedents which shew how they understood them, and how they practised them. Here we have the option either of declaring the *letter* of the precedents useless, or of conforming to it as an inspired interpretation of the law: we have adopted the latter, and are satisfied with our choice.

But is it true, that we can be at an "*immeasurable distance* from the *letter* of the apostolic precedent," while we are "in perfect harmony with its *spirit*." If so, we confess it is information. Again, if we are at an "*immeasurable distance* from the *letter* of the apostolic precedent," how is it that we " preposterously cling *to* that letter as a reason for refusing to go an inch farther"? This "immeasurable distance" has in a moment disappeared, and in the same sentence we are told, that, far as we were *from* the "letter of apostolic precedent," we still "preposterously cling *to*" it!

Our author proceeds, "they remain immoveable, to change the figure, not because they rest on any solid basis, but because they are suspended betwixt the *love of the brethren*, and the *remains of intolerance*; just as Mahomet's tomb is said to hang betwixt two magnets of equal powers in opposite directions." (*p.* 80, 81.) We will not offer any opinion respecting the assertion that we do not " rest on any solid basis," but as the force of what Mr. Hall says, is given us in " a *figure*," it is necessary to examine it. Two things had been mentioned immediately before, the *spirit*, and the *letter* of apostolic precedent; two things are mentioned in the "figure" under review, between which we are said to be " suspended," " the love of the brethren, and the remains of intolerance." *There* we are told that we " preposterously cling" to the letter of apostolic precedent; *here*, that one of the two magnets between which we are suspended is, " the remains of intolerance! What inference can we draw from these passages, except this, that it is *intolerant* to be attracted by apostolic precedent!

"The Scottish Baptists" are then brought forward by Mr. Hall (*p.* 81.), and he tells us they " act consistently." We suppose these are the same persons he had before called, "Sandemanian Baptists," who shelter themselves, " by a stern and consistent process of intolerance."(*p.*74.) He says,—" conceiving with Mr. K. that immersion on a profession of faith is a necessary introduction to the christian profession, they uniformly abstain from a participation in sacred offices with the members of other societies, and *without pretending to judge of their final state, treat them on* EVERY OCCASION *as men, whose religious pretensions are* DOUBTFUL." It is not necessary that we should defend the " Scottish Baptists,"—they are able to explain the reasons of their conduct, and they do not want the necessary talent, if they choose to come forward in their own defence. But one thing is manifest, the picture drawn by Mr. Hall is not a likeness: their own writings contradict what he thinks proper to say respecting them. Mr. McLEAN,* reciting an objection urged against his sentiments, says, " By making baptism a term of communion, you say, ' it becomes an occasion of dividing the real children of God.' We *freely admit that there are multitudes of God's dear children unenlightened as to baptism;* many of them have not attended to the subject; and others, through the influence of custom and false instruction, have seriously taken up with infant sprinkling in its stead.—We are grieved to think that so many of the *real children of God* are living in the neglect of the very first ordinance of the Gospel." &c.—Mr. WILLIAM BRAIDWOOD, one of the present pastors of the church with which *Mr. Mc Lean* was connected, says, " for my own part, I am not only persuaded that the Lord's people are in national churches, and *in the church of Rome itself*, but that they are all one in the faith of Jesus, and in subjection to his will.—They know in some essential leading particulars, the spiritual nature of Christ's kingdom; they love one another for the truth's sake; and they bring forth the fruits of righteousness."† Other testimonies might be

---

* In A Letter, intitled—Baptism must precede Church Fellowship; Works, vol. iii. p. 261, 262.—See also his Sermons, published by W. Jones, p. 99, 100, where the same sentiment occurs.

† Letters on a variety of subjects, relating chiefly to Christian Fellowship and Church Order.—12mo. p. 8.

added, but these it is presumed are sufficient. The reader can now judge of the accuracy of Mr. Hall's assertion respecting the "Scottish Baptists."

But why, it may be asked, should he attempt to involve them in this controversy?—Have they been intermeddling, and by this means brought down upon themselves the praise of consistency for their "stern process of intolerance?" Nothing of this nature is laid to their charge. But the reason is manifest: Mr. Hall intends by their means to inflict a deeper censure on us in England: and while they and we in some points are not agreed, his design is to involve us all in one common condemnation.

After the sentence on which the above remarks are made, our author adds, "whoever considers the import of the following passage, will be surprised Mr. Kinghorn should feel any hesitation in adopting the same system." Let us now observe his progress: he begins by an *inaccurate quotation*; "it is granted" says our author, that baptism is not expressly inculcated as a preparative to the Lord's supper, neither is it inculcated as a preparative *to any thing else*. But the first act of christian obedience is of course succeeded by the rest; and the required acknowledgment of our faith in Christ, in the nature of things, ought to *precede* the enjoyment of the privileges which arise from faith."—Whoever examines the work from which the above passage is quoted, will find that instead of the words '*to any thing else*,' which appear in Mr. Hall's work, the original terms are "*to any other duty or privilege separately considered.*" A difference sufficiently great, both in words and in meaning, to demand observation.

In commenting on this short paragraph, he says, the author "*designs to assert*, that such is the prescribed order of religious actions,—that unless that ordinance [baptism] is first attended to, *every other performance* is *invalid*; that whatever it may be in itself, not occupying its proper

place, it cannot lay claim to the *character of a duty*"!
Again, "He expressly tells us, that every other duty
must succeed, that is, come *after* baptism, which with respect to the Pædobaptists is impossible on our principles,
whence it necessarily follows, that while they retain their
sentiments, they are disqualified for the performance *of
duty*." Again, "The assertion he makes is in the form of
a general proposition, which is, that *all* the duties of
christianity must succeed baptism in contradiction to
going before it." (*p.* 82, 83.)

Our author adds, "thus much for the *duties;* let us
next hear what he says of the *privileges* of christianity.
Baptism, which he styles 'the required acknowledgment
of our faith in Christ,' he tells us 'ought to *precede* the
enjoyment of the privileges which arise from faith'. They
ought to precede, but *do* they in fact?* Is it *his* opinion
that all other sects, as a punishment for their disobedience
in one particular, are left destitute of the *spiritual immunities* which flow from faith? If it is not, it behoves him
to reflect on *the presumption* of such a mode of speaking,
which is *little less than arraigning the wisdom* of the great
head of the church, who dispenses his favours in a manner
so different from that *which he ventures to prescribe.*" (*p.*84.)
Of this dilemma, the first part does not follow from any
thing that I have said;—and, I thank God, the *impious
suggestion* insinuated in the second part, never entered my mind.

We have given Mr. Hall's interpretation at the above
length, that the reader may compare it with the original
paragraph in 'Baptism a term of Communion,' and see
whether such consequences can be drawn from it with the
most distant shadow of fairness. If, in addition to this
opportunity of comparison, he should refer to the other
parts of the work, and observe the general objects in view

---

* What he means by the expression, as it is here printed, "THEY *ought*
to precede," &c. we know not; but perhaps it was a grammatical oversight.

in the connection of the above quoted passage, we should scarcely think it necessary to add a single word, either of explanation or defence. But as some readers might deem such conduct an acknowledgment of Mr. Hall's interpretation, we will add few short observations.

Seldom has a more complete *misrepresentation* been exhibited to public view, or more pains taken to extract a meaning which was never thought of. The subject of discussion was NOT, in any part of it, whether those who differed from us on the subject of baptism *were*, or were *not* disqualified, either for the performance of duties or the enjoyment of privileges, in the sense in which Mr. Hall chooses to apply these words; but it so clearly related to the order, and connection of the external, visible, duties and privileges of the christian church, that it is surprising either a defence or explanation should be necessary. According to Mr. Hall's interpretation, we must have asserted that persons could not be christians if they were not baptised; but it is most manifest, that whenever the point in debate was stated, such an assertion was never either made or supposed; and *some other reason* must be found for Mr. Hall's remarks, different from the current of any sentiments which we expressed on the subject. To apply the terms "duty" and "privilege" in the manner he has done, might in his view answer a purpose; but for such a misapplication he alone is answerable.

If the reader turns to our former treatise, he will find that while that part of the subject which is now under review was in hand, on the very next page, there is a reply to an objection which some might make, as if we made baptism of more importance than it really is, and in which he will find, *not* a contradiction, as Mr. Hall thinks proper to assert (*p.* 88), but an explanation of the author's sentiments; and in fact a condensed recital of what he had stated in different parts of the work, "that the baptists frequently declare, that they do not consider baptism necessary to salvation; they do not depend upon it for their acceptance before God; nor do they view any as fit subjects for that ordinance, who are not previously believers in Christ, and justified in the sight of God by their faith." (*Baptism a term of Com. p.* 31.)

After such a declaration, made for the express purpose of obviating misapprehension, it is presumed no farther refutation of Mr. Hall's charges can be necessary.

The case of Cornelius is alleged, and Peter's admitting him and his household to all the "*privileges* of the church," is represented as decisive in the present controversy. Mr. Hall says, " the principle on which he [Peter] justified his conduct is plainly this, that when it is once ascertained that an individual is the object of divine acceptance, it would be impious to withhold from him any religious privilege." (*p.* 86, 87.)—Is not this the very principle on which we admit those, who we believe are objects of divine acceptance to baptism, if they have not been baptised before? " Until it be shewn that this was not the principle on which he rested his defence, or that the practice of strict communion is consistent with it, we shall feel ourselves compelled to discard with just detestation, a system of action which St. Peter contemplated with horror, as *withstanding God.* (*p.* 87.) But what did Peter command?—That they should be baptised. Would he not have been guilty of *withstanding God* if he had omitted this command? Would he have admitted them to the communion of the church without baptism? When it is proved, either that Peter *did* admit the house of Cornelius to the Lord's supper before they were baptised, or would have done so had they required it, it will be time enough to reconsider this "principle." In the mean while, we shall follow the order which Peter directed them to adopt, lest *we* should "*withstand God*" by neglecting to place one of the ordinances of his Gospel in its designed station, and to regard it for its proper end.—Here also we and Mr. Hall are completely at issue. In addition to all that he has said before, he tells us at the close of his paragraph, that the practice of strict communion "is replete with worse consequences, and is *far more offensive to God*, than that corruption of a christian ordinance to which it is opposed." (p. 87.) This explicit declaration clearly shews the tendency of Mr. Hall's sentiments. It seems then, that "a corruption" of a christian ordinance is a less evil than an adherence to the plan on which it was practised by inspired Apostles!—That though infant baptism is not according to the New Testament, but is confessed to be a "nullity," yet the adoption of the plan laid down in the apostolic writings is "*far more offensive to God* than the neglect of it; and that those who act upon it must be content to bear the blame of being "sinners above all men that dwell in Jerusalem." No wonder that Pædobaptists are so attached to Mr. Hall, they never met with such a baptist before!

"*This new doctrine*," adds Mr. Hall, "that the tenure by which religious privileges are held, is appropriated to the members of *one inconsiderable sect*, must strike the serious reader with astonishment. Are we in reality *the only persons who possess an interest in the common salvation?*" (p. 87.) Who has said we are? From our author's own book it is manifest that *we* have NOT said this: we have said the contrary. This "new doctrine" is a discovery of Mr. Hall's. The "doctrine" that baptism precedes in order and design, and ought to precede in fact the participation of the visible privileges of the christian church, is so far from being *new*, that it is as old as the apostolic commission, and has been so commonly and so universally admitted, that it is the *opposite doctrine* held by Mr. Hall that is *new*, and has been hitherto maintained by only an "inconsiderable" proportion of the christian community.

But the grand stroke which is to finish the business, is

reserved to the last part of the chapter, and terminates what Mr. Hall tells us, comprehends "all that is essential in the controversy." He asserts, that he has "examined with the utmost *care* and *impartiality* whatever our author has advanced in order to prove the necessary connection betwixt the two positive ordinances under consideration." (*p.* 92.) He had thought proper to say before, "we should be *extremely concerned* at imposing a false construction on his words;" (*p.* 82.) Let it be observed how these excellent and amiable qualities are displayed.

The charge now under review is this—"let it also be seriously considered, whether the positions we have been examining, do not coincide with the doctrine of the *opus operatum*, the opprobrium of the Romish church"! (*p.* 88.) These "positions," so pregnant with danger, Mr. Hall has discovered lurking in the sentence—" the first act of christian obedience is of course succeeded by the rest; and the required acknowledgment of our faith in Christ, in the nature of things, ought to precede the enjoyment of the privileges which arise from faith"! (*Baptism a term of Com. p.* 30.) Who would ever have suspected that here lay concealed the "*opus operatum*, the opprobrium of the Romish church"? We have already shewn that Mr. Hall's interpretation of the passage is not only contrary to the meaning we intended to convey, but contrary to the connection, and to the statements of the nature of the question at issue; so that it is not necessary to go over that ground again. Indeed the whole tenor of the argument in 'Baptism a term of Communion,' proceeded on principles so different from those which Mr. Hall professes to extract from the sentence now under his criticism, that it is no easy matter honourably to account for his misrepresentations.

In an examiner in the Inquisition, whose business it is to exert his acuteness in finding heresy where none was intended, and where by the fair construction of words none existed, such an accusation would have been in proper character: but in any other person, the display of such a talent does more injury to its possessor, than to him against whom it is exercised.

Whenever violent statements, not called for by any sufficient occasion, are exhibited, there must be some reason for it. Without pretending to say what that reason is in all its parts, one thing is evident; that notwithstanding the scorn with which Mr. Hall affects to treat the passages he has criticised, had they not been a serious obstacle in the way of his system, he never would have adopted the hazardous plan of pretending that they contained the *opus operatum* of popery!—But it was needful to dispose of them; we see how this was attempted, and the success of the experiment we leave to the decision of others.

SECTION V.

A Review of the general subject:—the amount of Mr. Hall's argument:—the advantage he gives to the Pædobaptists:—recapitulation of what has been conceded and proved:—consequences resulting from our author's system.

WE have thus endeavoured to follow Mr. Hall through his three first chapters. As the discussion has been long, a review may be of use, and can be given in few words.

Of the great principle laid down in ' Baptism a term of

Communion,' to which the reader's attention was distinctly and repeatedly directed as the turning point of a great part of the present controversy, Mr. Hall has said NOTHING.—Of the nature and constitution of the christian church, according to the New Testament directions and examples, to which also the reader's attention was directed as a subject of consequence in this inquiry, he has said NOTHING.—Of the scriptural *design* of baptism, on which it was distinctly stated the hinge of one material part of the debate turned, he has said NOTHING.—Of the purpose answered by baptism (except when an expression seems to have escaped him in a moment of forgetfulness) all that he has said amounts to NOTHING.—And his distortions, both of the statements and of the reasoning which he thought fit to notice, are *worse than* NOTHING. Whatever was the strength of the argument in the two first chapters of ' Baptism a term of Communion,' it remains *unimpaired*. Mr. Hall has busied himself by criticising incorrect quotations; by torturing expressions to obtain from them a sense which they were never intended to convey; and by caricaturing statements in order that he might make them hideous: but he has avoided the principal parts of the argument which were directed against his system, and (whatever were his reasons) has left them in all their force!

Whatever can be called argument in Mr. Hall's book proceeds on the practical absurdity of supposing that the *unbaptised* can, in that character, have a right to communion. The discussion occasioned by this controversy must always come to the inquiry; which is to give way— the *old* system of apostolic times, or the *new* system of Mr. Hall? No reasoning can prove the two plans to be alike drawn from the word of God; and in vain we pretend to make it our rule, if we neglect the plan there laid down in precept and illustrated by examples, and adopt another not contained in it.

Every one must have observed how eagerly Pædobaptists have pleaded Mr. Hall's authority in their own favour. They see that he has lowered the practical obligation to obey the law of baptism, and thus made a concession which they can improve. They clearly perceive that if we are vulnerable on that side, they gain an advantage which nothing else could give them. Pædobaptists who think baptism (as they view it) is of any importance, must laugh at the inconsistency of those who would introduce into the church persons who are declared to be *unbaptised;* and say, see what these Baptists are driven to concede! With all their zeal about a divine institution—all their appeals to primitive christianity—and all their boast of "overwhelming evidence," so conscious are they that their system is of no practical consequence, that they will admit those who have had no baptism at all!

Mr. Hall has CONCEDED that in the apostolic church baptism *was* a term of communion—*was* a term of profession,—that the Apostle Paul *did* allude to the two christian ordinances, so that they were both together in his mind,— that his expressions were correct, as they were addressed to a society which consisted *only of Baptists,*—and that there is a "*natural order*" in the christian institutions. It has also been *proved* that this "order" appears, first in the apostolic commission; next in the apostolic conduct; that nothing can reverse this "order"; that every view which we can take of the design of baptism, according to the New Testament statements, shews us, that it *naturally* preceded the Lord's supper;—and that no church can receive a person who is unbaptised, according to the rule of the New Testament.

Since then, on the one hand it has been *granted,* and on the other *proved,* that both the *command* and *design* of baptism shew "the *natural order* of the christian sacraments", was this "order" the effect of *accident,* or of *design?* None will say that it was the effect of *accident;*

M

and if it was the result of *design*, what right have we to alter an established, and *designed* order?

If then we had no farther information, than that in *this order* the commission of our Lord placed his own institutions, and in *this order* the Apostles constantly administered them, we ought to follow it; or else, it should be proved that there was *no design* in the arrangement—that our Lord intended that, in succeeding times, men might *first* become members of his church and remember his death and *then* profess their faith in him by their baptism, or pursue a different course as accident might lead them. It should be proved that the Apostles *did* act on this plan, or would have acted upon it in circumstances like ours, and then we will allow that the question is at rest; but till this is done, it will be impossible to give a satisfactory reason for NOT keeping the ordinances *as* they were delivered to us. The order used in the administration of the Lord's supper, first breaking and distributing the bread, and then handing round to the communicants the wine, stands on evidence precisely of the same kind with that which is now under consideration; and Mr. Hall might change this order, and plead with as much reason, for any alteration that he might wish to introduce, as for administering it to persons professedly unbaptised.

If the New Testament was intended to be a *rule*, and an *inspired* rule, it is binding in its obligation. But do we obey its injunctions if we adopt a line of conduct directly contrary to all the directions and examples which this *inspired rule* exhibits? Here, then, we take our station, and we contend that the plan of requiring baptism previous to communion, is justified both by the natural interpretation of the commission delivered by the Lord, and by the whole weight of apostolic example.

If in following such authority we go astray, we are misled by inspired teachers; *infallible* guides have guided us *wrongly:* and our duty is to take care lest we follow

Christ and the Apostles too exactly: the rule which they have given us is not *sufficient*; for where it appears the most precise, we shall err if we adopt it! On this plan it is in vain to look to the *New Testament* for the pattern of the christian church: the nearer we conform to it, the farther we shall be from truth; and our error will arise from imagining that we are bound to place the institutions of the Lord in the order in which he himself had arranged them. If it can be proved that this order is erroneous, let it be done; but if this cannot be effected, let us remember, that we are far more likely to err by deviating from inspired precedents, or practically setting aside a divine command, than by submitting our weak and often wandering reasonings to that plain rule, which was laid down by him, " in whom are hid all the treasures of wisdom and knowledge."

But then it is said, here is a "*new case*": if so, either this "case" must be adjudged by the *old* rule, or it requires a *new* rule. If no such rule can be found, we have no authority to make one; and the case must be decided by the law and precedents which are already recorded. If the "new case" is to set aside obedience to an express direction, we make the New Testament like the statute books of the realm, which contain laws that are obsolete, and which it would be a shame to enforce.

We shall now proceed to examine some of Mr. Hall's observations and reasonings on other parts of this controversy. This however we intend to do with brevity. Many of them are mere misrepresentations; many have nothing to do with the subject before us; but none which we conceive to be of vital consequence shall be passed over.

CHAPTER V.

ON DISPENSING WITH A CHRISTIAN ORDINANCE.

THE chapter concerning "the charge of dispensing with a christian ordinance", is marked with peculiar infelicities. It is not more distinguished by the gentler features of the christian character than those which preceded it; it is not superior in its reasoning, or in that fairness which *first* ascertains the sense and bearing of an opponent's argument, and *then* tries its strength; nor is it remarkable for the accuracy of its quotations, of which there may be occasion to adduce instances.

Mr. Hall seizes an opportunity of finding fault with me for saying, that I apprehended the expression 'dispensing power' was suggested by a circumstance in English History, when Charles II. granted Dissenters an indulgence beyond the then existing law. He accuses me of falling into an error, and is surprised that I should not know that the doctrine of dispensation was familiar to preceding ages. (*p.* 96.) If on this point I had been in an error, it would have been of no consequence to the debate; it was a matter of opinion; it occurred in an illustration which I gave of my own view of the sense of the expression in question; if it was a mistake, the argument would still have remained where it was before, and the conjecture that had been hazarded, would have been thrown aside among thousands more of the same kind.

But an attentive reader will observe that I said nothing respecting the "doctrine of dispensation." I knew the Popes had claimed it, and Mr. Hall is correct in stating that they assumed a power of this nature to a great extent. The "error" at which he pretends to be surprised, is an "error" of his own. That which was stated was, what appeared to be the occasion which brought the *expression* " dispensing power" into common currency.

Though Mr. Hall thinks proper to find fault, he does not shew that I was wrong, by proving that the *expression* was in common use *before* the period mentioned. After it had been brought forward in a marked manner in parliament, it became familiar, especially to those who were interested in the discussions then in debate. It was therefore often recited in the detail of events which concerned the Dissenters, and was circulated through the general body. By this means, as a well known phrase, it came into use in theological controversy, and has been employed by Mr. Booth and others in the present inquiry.

I shall now leave it with the reader to judge how far I was justified in stating *what* I did, and in stating it *as* I did: namely, that "the *expression* 'dispensing power'—was suggested, *I apprehend*, by a circumstance in English History." (*Bap. a term of Com. p.* 90.)

Unwilling either to equivocate, or to encourage equivocation under the shelter of ambiguous language, an explanation was given, and we stated *what*, in our view *was* exercising a dispensing power, and what was *not*. The reader will find it in p. 90, 91, of our former treatise, but he will neither find *it*, nor any reference to it, in Mr. Hall's Reply, but on the contrary a repetition of his own remark, that this argument owed its force to the "equivocal use of terms." (*p.* 100.) In strict justice, therefore, this part of his book might be passed over.

But as he has thought fit to bring this part of the discussion forward again, a few observations may not be deemed unnecessary. He says, the exercise of a dispensing power "always implies a *known* and *conscious* departure from the law." He who claims such a power, "asserts a right to deviate from the letter of legal enactments." (*p.* 97.) Hence our author denies that he lays claim to a dispensing power. "So remote," he says, "is our practice from implying the claim of superiority to law, that it is in our view, the necessary result of obedience to that comprehensive precept, 'receive ye one another even as Christ has received you to the glory of the Father'." He then adds, " if the practice of toleration is admitted at all, it must have for its object some supposed deviation from truth, or failure of duty; and as there is no transgression where there is no law, and every such deviation must be opposed to a rule of action, if the forbearance exercised towards it is assuming a dispensing power, the accusation equally lies against all parties, except such as insist upon an absolute uniformity." (*p.* 100.)

Comparing these passages together, it necessarily follows, that he who *dispenses* with a law, and he who *tolerates* those who have not fulfilled "a duty of perpetual obligation", (*p.* 98,) are, to say the least, in very similar circumstances. In both cases it is admitted that there is a law, that the law is in force, that the law is not obeyed, and that he whose deficiency of obedience is acknowledged —is notwithstanding received, and placed in precisely the same situation as if he had obeyed it. The facts are the same in both cases; and if, according to Mr. Hall, we ought not to claim the power of *dispensing* with the law, we can yet go quite as far, by *tolerating* those who do not obey it. But since he pleads for a toleration of such extent, that an acknowledged positive command can be passed by, as if it was either of no force or of no use, we ask, what precept enjoins, and what example warrants a toleration of this kind? Or, if we admit analogies, where can our author find a single instance, in which *any* direct injunction of Christ was omitted, for the purpose of opening a door to those who otherwise would not enter? The importance of New Testament toleration we fully admit, and would not knowingly narrow the system on which the Apostles acted; but it has not yet been proved, that either their instructions, or their example, authorise us in breaking down the precepts which were raised by the authority of the head of the church.

But says Mr. Hall, " we contend that the law is *in our favour*." (*p.* 98.) If so, it is both needless and delusive to plead for the unbaptised on the ground of *toleration ;* for that term supposes that there is a *known* and *acknowledged* deficiency in their conduct, contrary to the meaning of some existing law ; but if there is a posterior law which allows their admission, they should be introduced on the broad basis of law ; the paragraph containing the law should be read at the church-meeting on their being proposed, and entrance demanded for them on its authority. Where, however, is this law to be found? It was evidently not the intention of the original law to admit the unbaptised, nor was this considered to be its meaning, when it was "perfectly understood." We ask then, what subsequent *Act of Toleration* has passed into a law for the relief of those who do not obey the primitive statute ; and when did such an Act receive the *Royal Assent?*

Our author brings forward the supposed authority of a "comprehensive precept—receive ye one another, even as Christ received you to the glory of the Father." But this precept, by our author's own confession, was addressed to persons already in the church, and not to those who had not been admitted. How then can this " comprehensive precept" include those who were not comprehended in it?

Our author talks about forbearance : an excellence of a distinguished class, which we wish to cultivate, to all the extent recorded or required in the New Testament. But what is the *forbearance* enjoined in that volume ? Is it forbearing to require what Christ required by positive appointment ? If it is, where is this forbearance commanded ? Let one instance of the kind be produced, and the system may then be carried to an interminable extent. If no such specimen can be found, and no law requiring such a disregard of a previously existing statute can be discovered, the forbearance required in the New Testament cannot be urged in opposition to our practice; for of all the faults which were the subjects of reproof, we never find the primitive church rebuked for standing fast, and holding the traditions which they had been taught whether by word or apostolic epistle, (2 *Thess.* ii. 15.)

Our author says, " in every controversy, the medium of proof by which a disputed point is attempted to be disproved, should contain something distinct from the position itself, or no progress is made." (*p.* 102.) This is granted: and had he attended to his own remark, the discussion would have been in a more advanced state. Had he canvassed the first leading principle presented to his notice, that according to the New Testament baptism was intended to be a mark of connection with the christian church—had he shewn us what was the *design* of that ordinance—had he investigated the constitutional principles of a christian church according to the scriptures—to all which his attention was directed; there would have been mediums of proof brought forward, which might have been applied to the present discussion: but he thought proper to take a different course.

" Near akin to this is the charge of "*sanctioning*" a corruption of a sacred ordinance." (*p.* 103.) By the tenor of this sentence and the inverted commas before and after the word *sanctioning*, the reader will suppose Mr. Hall is quoting something from our treatise. But from what part?--no reference to the page is given, nor indeed any hint whereby the place can be discovered. If the reader takes Mr. Hall's word for it, he may go on without any further trouble; but if he wishes to see how the supposed quotation stands, and of what words it is composed, besides that one, (" sanctioning") which Mr. Hall has marked, he must take considerable pains to obtain satisfaction. In time he will be convinced that no such passage as that which Mr. Hall professes to quote *exists!* Where he obtained it we know not. The participle, *sanctioning,* we believe is never used except in quoting our author's own words (*see Baptism a term, &c. p.* 56): the verb to *sanction*, is used a few times; but in no instance that we can find, have we laid down such a proposition as Mr. H. has brought forward, and of course we need not support it.*

The succeeding paragraph brings forward another passage, which Mr. Hall thinks fit to inform his reader, "is marked in Italics, and delivered with the solemnity of an oracle"—and—" *is characterised by the same spirit of extravagance.*" Here we are on safer ground, the page is referred to ; but the reader will find two errors in the quotation! Our words were, " the supposition itself, that toleration and forbearance will justify us in allowing an omission of a law of Christ in his church, operates as a repeal of that law; and introduces a rule of action which would generally be deemed unreasonable." (*Baptism a term of Communion, p.* 53.)

In the next paragraph Mr. Hall says " he illustrates his assertion by referring to the legal qualification required in a candidate for a seat in Parliament." (*Reply p.* 105, 106.) If the reader examines for himself, he will find that it is *another* " assertion" which is illustrated in the passage referred to; we therefore dismiss Mr. Hall's observation on this illustration without farther notice.

* When we have no reference we are left to conjecture; in *Baptism a term of Communion, p.* 64, it is said, "The Protestants and Protestant Dissenters refuse to unite with Roman Catholics and the Establishment, because in so doing, they would *sanction* what they believe are corrupt appendages to the law of the Saviour. The strict Baptist refuses to admit those whom he considers as unbaptised, because in so doing he would *sanction* the *omission* of an express part of the law itself." Could this be what Mr. Hall intended to quote? If so, it contains no such proposition as he adduces: but we have had instances of a similar mistake before.

But as he returns to the former proposition, which he says is *"untenable"*, we will attend briefly to his objections. He attempts to set the Apostle Paul in opposition to our statement; and could he succeed, we should have a more formidable opponent to deal with than any who has yet appeared. But the Apostle has *not* supported Mr. Hall's theory, nor is the passage quoted to his point. His meaning is—the Apostle censured the backbitings, whisperings, swellings, tumults, in the Corinthian church; —here was an omission of a law of Christ;—yet the Apostle did not intimate "an intention to *exclude*" the offenders—therefore, on the principle which we had laid down, Mr. Hall says, "he was guilty of repealing the commands of God." *(p.* 107.)

Now, it is granted that backbitings and other evils did exist; and it is granted also, that those who were guilty of them did omit a part of the law of Christ; but they were evils which the Apostle was labouring to rectify, and which he was determined should not continue. Before the existence of such evils becomes a parallel case to the admission of the unbaptised, these backbiters, whisperers, &c. should be *admitted in that character:* they must be supposed to have said, that the terms of communion which some people pleaded for, were far *too strict;* that they were not convinced by any thing they had heard that backbiting was a crime; and that they wished to come to the Lord's table notwithstanding they indulged themselves in this gratification. It must be supposed also, that the liberal Corinthians received them on that ground, and that they were so attached to the system of mixed communion, that they declared backbiting and whispering, &c. were no bar to communion. This supposition is necessary, or the case of the lamented imperfections of these Corinthians will not apply as a reason why a known law of Christ should be set aside in his church. Nor is it correct that the Apostle did not give the slightest intimation of an intention to "*exclude*" them. His wish was to reduce them to repentance; hence he intreated them to consider their ways; he expressed his fears that they would be found such as he would not, and that God would humble him among them, by bringing to light the evil tempers and evil conduct of those who he once hoped were better characters. But he was coming the third time—the affair should be investigated—in the mouth of two or three witnesses should every word be established; and he gave the offenders solemn warning by saying, "I told you before, and foretell you as if I were present the second time; and being absent, now I write to them which heretofore have sinned, and to all other, that if I come again *I will not spare*. (*See* 2 *Cor.* xii. 20, 21. and xiii. 1, 2.) Such a threatening clearly intimated, that those who did not repent might expect from the Apostle a discipline, of which their exclusion from communion would be the smallest part.

The proposition which Mr. Hall criticises, and which he says is full of mistakes, is not only plain in its application to the case before us, but it is *true;* what he has said about it is merely a perversion of its obvious and intended meaning. View the proposition in its respective parts;—it supposes that Jesus Christ has given us laws for the regulation of his church at large; it supposes also that the plea of toleration and forbearance was urged by some as a reason why one of these laws should be omitted. If in consequence of such a plea *that* law *was* omitted, and the church which acted on this plan received members who neither *had* obeyed that law, nor ever *intended* to do so; they then pursued exactly the same course as if the law was virtually repealed; and their making toleration and forbearance reasons why they omitted the law, was a practical declaration that such reasons were, in their view, sufficient to suspend its operation. How then can it be denied, that such reasoning, as far as it had influence, would *eventually operate as a repeal of the law*? It was in fact saying, Jesus Christ, it is true, *did* enact such a law, but the state of things was in his time different from what it is now ; we have maturely considered the point, and have concluded, that obedience to the law ought not now to be required. Here the law of Christ is omitted by a *deliberate act*, and in consequence of reasoning which it is supposed will justify it. Whenever this is the case, as it must be in every instance in which Baptists plead for the introduction of persons professedly unbaptised, the law of baptism, as a law given for the regulation of his church, is treated as if it was actually *repealed*, and placed in the same situation as if the Lord himself had declared, that though baptism was once essential to communion, it is now necessary no longer.

After this explanation, which is nothing more than calling the reader's attention to the terms and evident meaning of the proposition, it will not be necessary to refute what Mr. Hall calls a "*mistake*," namely, " By affirming that to endure *under any circumstances* the omission of a rule of action, is to repeal it, he has reduced the very conception of toleration to an impossibility." *(p.* 108.) If Mr. H. means that this sentence expresses the sense of our proposition, it is a "*mistake*" of his own.

He thinks the errors and evils of the Corinthians exhibit such a proof of toleration as admits of no reply. But there is no similarity between Paul's conduct towards the Corinthians, and the admission of communion with the unbaptised. Mr. Hall pleads for the *admission* of those who *deny* that baptism is obligatory, or who have no other baptism than that which he denominates *a nullity :* and he would say, admit them into the church notwithstanding this, and even though you never expect to see them change either their opinion or their practice. The Apostle Paul did *not* plead for the *admission* of those who *denied* that they ought to be sober, just, and temperate; but when they shewed, by displaying their evil passions, that they were not what he expected, he lamented over them and reproved them. But, says Mr. Hall, these evils did "not prevent his forbearance". How he forbore with them we have already seen: whilst absent he wrote an epistle, in which he warned and exhorted them; but he told them, that he intended to visit them, and that when he was present he would *not spare*. Would Mr. Hall advise the ministers of mixed churches to adopt such language; and if they did, what would be the consequence? The cases which he attempts to identify have no similarity. The Apostles would judge whether the profession of faith made by those who offered themselves for baptism, was, or was not sufficient, and whether the fruits which they brought forth were, or were not meet for repentance. When churches were formed, and left to act on the principles which the Apostles had laid down, the ministers and members of which they were composed, would naturally determine whether the candidates for fellowship had a just claim on their attention; and they would equally judge, whether their conduct in after life did, or did not support that claim. But then it should be remembered, that they were admitted into the church on the ground, that they were ready to obey the laws of Christ; not on the avowed principle, that though some of these laws not only were *not* obeyed, but were *not intended* to be obeyed, still they might be received with as much cordiality as if they had obeyed them all. Yet *this* is the principle which Mr. Hall would have us to adopt; and he thinks it strange that we will not acknowledge that this was Paul's principle of forbearance with the Corinthians!

Mr. Hall says, *(p.* 110.) " the πρωτον ψευδος, the radical fallacy of the whole proceeding, consists in confounding our interpretation of the law, however just, with the law itself: in affirming of the first whatever is true of the last;

and of *subverting under that pretext the right of private judgment.*" The first part of this sentence is explained by Mr. Hall himself in the following words; "the interpretation of a rule is, to him who adopts it, equally binding with the rule itself, because every one must act on his own responsibility". He then, who deliberately thinks, that the only conclusion deducible from the law of baptism is, that it ought to precede communion, must on Mr. Hall's own concession, require baptism before the reception of the Lord's supper. Thus far we agree. Our author proceeds—"but he has no authority whatever to bind it on the conscience of his brother, and to treat him who receives it not, as though he were at issue with the legislator." Had he stopped here we should have said, thus far also we coincide : we address the reasons which weigh with us, both to the understandings and consciences of men. We are conscious we ought to go no farther, nor have we any right to use any other means "to bind" the consciences of others, than exhibiting what binds our own : and as to our conduct towards those who do not agree with us in our views, we allow that we ought not to treat them harshly ; we hope we do not :—we believe that many of them are good men, though we think them mistaken. But it is added—"it is this *presumptuous claim of infallibility,* this *assumption of the prerogative of Christ,* this disposition to *identify ourselves with him,* and to place our conclusions on a footing with his mandates, that is the secret spring of all that *intolerance* which has so long bewitched the world with her sorceries, from the elevation of papal Rome, where she thunders and lightens from the Vatican, down to BAPTIST *Societies,* where she whispers feebly from the dust"!(*p.*110,111.)

Here we cannot help asking, what does this mean? "This presumptuous claim of infallibility"! What "claim" is that; and who makes it? If this "claim" is ascribed to those who maintain that the New Testament requires baptism to precede communion, the only inference that we can draw is, that according to our author's mode of reasoning, though such persons may *think*, they must neither *speak* their opinion, nor *act* upon it. For if they unite together as a church on their own principles, and declare, this we believe *to be according to the law of Christ*, and we do not think proper to *break it* by admitting the unbaptised, they are open to all the violent charges which are here urged against them. They are, however, furnished with a reply in Mr. Hall's own words; " whether it be true or not, that we are commanded to act thus, such is our opinion; and *with this persuasion we are not at liberty to act in a different manner."* (*p.* 116.)

Besides, the charge may be retorted ; if Mr. Hall could form his church on his own principles, would he not think it right to do so? If he did, would not the terms of communion with his church be, the admission, that the unbaptised have a right of access to the Lord's table?—and if so, would not *he* "bind" his "interpretation" on the conscience of his brethren; since many of those who did not think him correct, could not join with him? In forming his own church on this plan, he would act on what he conceived was the will of Christ; and what do his opponents do more? But the absurdity of such charges is their best refutation. As to the contemptuous language in which BAPTIST *Societies* are spoken of, may God preserve all who compose *them* from treating the meanest of their christian brethren in such a manner!

CHAPTER VI.

MR. HALL'S MISREPRESENTATIONS OF THE ARGUMENT RESPECTING THE GROUND OF DISSENT EXPOSED.

THE first thing that should be done in any controversy is to understand what the argument of an opponent is. If this plain position is granted, we need not say much in reply to Mr. Hall's fifth chapter.

The stale trick of making bad syllogisms, and attempting to pass them off as containing the arguments of another party, which occupies the first part of this chapter, is not worthy of notice; and the point of the reasoning which a churchman is supposed to use against the patron of mixed communion, in chapter viii. of Baptism a term of Communion, Mr. Hall has not thought proper to meet.

The argument in that chapter is, that the Baptists have a ground of their own, distinct from that held in common with other nonconformists, and which by a clear and brief argument, justifies their dissent from the Establishment, in consequence of the view they take of the nature of a christian church, and of the description which the New Testament gives of its members: but that on the plan adopted in the Establishment, a class of members is systematically introduced into the church of a description so different from that in the sacred volume, as to form a body of a distinct nature. According to the doctrine of the Establishment, infants are made members of the church in their baptism; and except in extreme cases, remain such all their days. According to the New Testament, those who became members of the church, first believed, were baptised on the profession of their faith, and then were added to the church. The strength of the arguments urged by the Baptist against the Churchman, it was observed, consisted in the *directions* of Christ, the *examples* of the Apostles, and the *precedents* set before us by the Apostolic church in the New Testament.

It was stated, that however a churchman might be perplexed by arguments derived from such sources, yet if he discovered that his opponent would admit to communion those who had never been baptised, he might retort, that this was taking a liberty with the injunctions of Jesus Christ which *he* never thought of doing. That he did not OMIT or practically *disannul the authority of* ANY injunction, which he believed was of *perpetual obligation;* that if the precept respecting forbearance is pleaded on the one side, and if this is sufficient to set aside the operation of an ordinance still in force, the spirit of the injunction respecting ' *order*', will surely justify the other party in pleading for the practices of the Establishment respecting those points on which nothing is commanded in scripture.

The churchman's defence proceeds on the principle, that the acknowledged *omission* of one of the ordinances of Christ, is a *greater departure* from the New Testament, than the appointment of those rites and ceremonies, which he does not pretend to place on the ground of divine command, but which were adopted by his church at the Reformation, and are still continued, as desirable (in his view) for the preservation of decency and order.

To the general design of this reasoning nothing like a reply is attempted. Particular expressions are found fault with; some strange mistakes are made; and other things are so misrepresented, that, from Mr. Hall's statements, no person, however acute, would ever conceive what had been urged by his opponent.

He thinks proper to state the case thus: "if the members of the Establishment inquire on what ground do you receive a Pædobaptist, we reply, because we are *expressly commanded* to receive him. But if we inquire in our turn, why do you kneel at the Sacrament, is it affirmed that they will reply in the same manner?" *(p. 117.)*

We are *expressly commanded* to receive a *Pædobaptist*—says Mr. Hall: let him prove this point, and we grant, the debate will be ended. But will he inform us whether we are *expressly commanded* to receive him as baptised or as *un*baptised? If the former, then the controversy concerning *baptism* is finished; for it would be absurd to assert that believers ought to be immersed in the name of Christ, (which Mr. Hall does in express terms, *p.* 98) if we are commanded to receive a person who has only been sprinkled in his infancy as a baptised person. If he says we are *expressly commanded* to receive a Pædobaptist as *un*baptised, the Churchman would reply, and with good reason, this is DISSENTING *indeed*, not only from our establishment, but from the primitive church itself, and even from that pattern which our opponents acknowledge was drawn by the finger of the Lord! He would add, that *he* acknowledged *two* ordinances in the church; but was not inclined to adopt a system which supposed that Christ began with *two*, but designed to end with *one:* and if the principles of the New Testament were of so lax and compliant a nature, that they would not support in its authority an institution which the Lord himself had appointed, it would be impossible to prove that they would condemn him for conforming to ceremonies, the end of which was not the subversion of any divine institution, but only the promotion of peace and unity.

"But", he says, "do the Pædobaptists when they propose to commune with us, expect us to join with them in their practice . . infant baptism?" *(p. 121.)* We grant they do not; but if we agree to their proposal, they justly infer, either that we allow the validity of their baptism, which Mr. Hall tells us is a "*nullity*"; or that baptism is not required in the New Testament previous to communion; or else, that the law which once required it, is become a dead letter, and no longer claims the observance that was formerly its due. None of these concessions are we prepared to make. Separate from the opposition which one of them makes to our sentiments as Baptists, we esteem their spirit and tendency *subversive* of those principles by which the cause of primitive christianity is to be promoted.

Occasion has occurred before of noticing Mr. Hall's *accuracy;* and this chapter presents us with additional specimens. Observe what he lays to our charge:—" He *largely* insists on the superiority of his system to ours, on account of its being *at a greater remove* from the principles of the established church. ' *The strict Baptist,*' he observes, ' can set the churchman at defiance', &c." (*Reply, p.* 121, 122.) Here the reference is to Baptism a term of Communion, p. 127. What we *did* state the reader will find in p. 127, 128, of our former work. He will there see, that the position laid down was, that we *as Baptists* had a visible and forcible reason (arising from our views of baptism) for leaving the Establishment, in addition to the motives operating on dissenters in general. For on the supposition that we were right in our ideas of that ordinance, the inference was clear, that the established church is wrong in its constitution; its members are of a different class from those who were members of the primitive church, and they are united together in a way different from that appointed by the Saviour. This one consideration, it was observed, settled the great question in the controversy, which is, whether the established church, taken in the aggregate amount, is not of a different character from that body which is in the New Testament called the church of Christ? And it was farther observed, that (though we allow there are other grounds of dissent, yet) nothing had such a tendency to give the established church that peculiarity of character which compelled our dissent, as its baptism. Such is the general outline of the statement; it is misrepresented; it is caricatured; half a sentence is taken, without regard to the meaning of the whole, for the purpose of making what was said appear ridiculous; but it is *not* disproved.

Besides, Mr. Hall reasons from his own inaccurate quotation: with the formality of inverted commas, and a reference to the page, he professes to copy the words "*the strict Baptist* can set the Churchman at defiance," &c. (*Reply, p.* 122); but if the reader turns to the passage, he will find that we did *not* say "the *strict* Baptist":—that our argument, in that paragraph, did not suppose either that "the Baptist" was strict or *not* strict. He was brought forward merely in the character of a *Baptist* defending himself on his own ground: and on that ground which is common to Baptists at large. But it was observed in the succeeding paragraph, that if he quitted his strong hold of scripture direction and precedent, he would then lay himself open to objections for want of consistency; that the Churchman would be in a difficulty when he met him as *a Baptist*, but would press him with a powerful objection if he found him a disciple of Mr. Hall.

A quotation from Bishop Hall's 'Apologie against Brownists,' is next the object of our opponent's censure, and the good Prelate's mode of reasoning is called 'futile.' (*p.* 127.) He clearly saw that a society without baptism (such a society as might be formed on Mr. Hall's theory), was *not* a church with a constitution according to the New Testament; but, he contended, that a christian assembly which did possess the baptism required in the Gospel, was *a church*, though it might contain many errors, and needed to be reformed: and he defended the Reformation, not because the church of Rome was, in his view, *not* a church, but because it was a *corrupt* church, and it was therefore necessary to leave that society for the sake of greater conformity to the primitive standard. "This," he says, " is our case, we did not make a *new* church, but mended an old". (*Apol. p.* 533. § 6.) Other authorities from the same treatise might be quoted, were it needful, in illustration of the opinion which the Bishop expressed in the short passage which we had copied. The Bishop was opposing Pædobaptist "Separatists," who objected to the church of England because of its *constitution.* Some of this number had fled to Amsterdam on account of the persecution at home, and a party of Baptists rose up among them who had not long before urged, that neither the "Separatists" nor the Establishment had the true constitution of a christian church, because the baptism of both these bodies was (to use Mr. Hall's term) " *a nullity.*" The last mentioned opinion had been boldly brought forward by *Mr. John Smyth,* in a pamphlet entitled, " *The character of the Beast, or the false constitution of the Church discovered;*" printed in 1609. The Bishop had this pamphlet before him, and quoted it in his 'Apologie'; but as it was *another* pamphlet written by *Pædobaptists* that was the more immediate object of his attack, he did not enter into a detailed opposition to Mr. Smyth's arguments. Against the *Pædobaptists* he urged, that they could not deny the constitution of the Established church, since they allowed the validity of its baptism; but if they still insisted that the Establishment had no constitution, he told them that they "*must goe forward to Anabaptisme.*" This is the outline of his reasoning on this part of the subject; and when it is viewed in connection with the state of the controversy at that time, it will instantly appear, that nothing Mr. Hall has said, amounts to the shadow of a proof, that the good Bishop was wrong. Our author deduces an inference from the Bishop's words, which doubtless in his esteem is valid, but it needs no refutation, because it has no concern with the Bishop's proposition.*

In addition to the attack made on us through the medium of Bishop Hall, we are led back to some observations on the *Reformation,* which occur in Baptism a term of Communion, p. 55. Mr. Hall thinks fit to say, "Not satisfied with asserting that our principles militate against the lawfulness of Dissent, he maintains that they are inconsistent with protestantism, and that by necessary consequence they convict LUTHER and his associates of *schism* and *rebellion.*" (*Reply, p.* 127.) He then quotes a passage from the page above mentioned; he leaves out a part of the paragraph which is of consequence to the conclusion that was drawn from the whole; begins his reasoning from these imperfect premises, and ends by professing that he has "detected"—"palpable sophistry."

Mr. Hall calls our argument "nugatory," (*p.* 129.) but in the first place, let us inquire what it is. It was stated that "if we had no right to refuse" the communion of good men "with us, till they conform to what we are convinced is the will of Christ, we had no right to leave them because they deviated from his will. The ground in both cases is the same. Once take away the obligation of conforming to the will of Christ, and the REFORMATION is

---

* Mr. Hall says,—"if the reasoning extolled by Mr. K. is just, he [Bishop Hall] was guilty of *schism,* in refusing to unite at one and the same time with **Heretics, Roman Catholics,** and **Dissenters!**" (*p.* 127.) Such an inference has no connection with the Bishop's sentiments. With his views, he would have said to each of the above parties, I leave you, not because your churches have *no* constitutional principles; for you all maintain the christian ordinance of baptism, and you each have a portion of truth: but I leave you because you maintain so many tenets which I think wrong, that I cannot hold communion with you; and since I leave you for the *truth's* sake, I fear not the charge of *schism.* But if he had found among any of the above parties some who opposed the necessity of baptism, it is fairly to be inferred from his own statements, that he would have told *them,* that if ever he and they had communion on earth, they must first be initiated into the church by baptism.

declared a mischievous insurrection, in which all protestants are included in aiding and abetting a needless and schismatical project." So far Mr. Hall quotes the words we had used. "But," it is added, "if it be right to leave good men, because they have left Jesus Christ, it is right not to admit them till they come to HIS TERMS. If this be not granted, we have to place the Reformation from popery, and our dissent from the Establishment of our country, on a basis entirely new; and a basis very different from the obligation to obey the will of Christ, as expressed in the New Testament; for the law of the Lord, and the practice of the primitive church, are not to be accounted our standard." (*Bap. a term of Com. p.* 55.)

The latter part of the above paragraph, which Mr. Hall omits, furnishes a sufficient reply to his reasonings. Neglecting the evident design of the preceding argument, he says, "if he means that we are obliged to demand in others a *perfect compliance* with his will, as a term of communion, he takes away the possibility of toleration." (*Reply, p.* 128, 129.) Here our author changes the proposition. If we ask for no more than that men *come to Christ's terms,* are *his* terms liable to this charge? Is there any intolerance in requiring nothing more than the terms which the LORD required? If, according to the supposition which Mr. Hall has made, *Luther* admitted a Roman Catholic to communion in his church, did he not admit him on this very ground, that he believed the Catholic acceded to *Christ's terms?* If our author should admit a churchman, would it not be on the same supposition? But here the question returns, what are these terms? When *Christ* made them known to his disciples, baptism was one of them; let it be shewn that this part of his appointment is *abrogated,* and we will agitate the present controversy no longer.

Mr. Hall concludes his chapter by professing to retort the argument, and to remind us " of the striking resemblance between the system of strict communion, and that which is maintained by the churches of England and Rome." (*Reply, p.* 131.) His first charge is the old reproach about "the assumption of infallibity." If he is correct, we and the members of the church of Rome claim it alike. But if that church had never done more than we do, the debates concerning her infallibility would never have existed. The principles on which every Baptist church we ever knew, avowedly act, are so diametrically opposite to those of the Catholic community, that it is surprising any man should say, they are the same. The Roman Catholic church maintains that the scripture is *not* the sole rule of faith—that men have *not* the right to judge of it for themselves, and form their religious opinions and practice from it; for this (the Catholics assert) is a most pernicious maxim; it destroys all obedience to the church which we are commanded to hear.* Where will Mr. Hall find any protestants of *any party* who will adopt such maxims as these?

What can he mean by the insinuation—"when not satisfied with this (i. e. confining baptism to adults) he *insists upon forcing his interpretation on the conscience of his brother*, and treats him precisely in the same manner as though he avowedly contradicted Christ, and his Apostles, what is this but an assumption of infallibity?" (*p.* 132.) Is our saying to those whom Mr. Hall acknowledges are not baptised—we believe that the church should be composed only of persons who are baptised, and for this reason we cannot receive you—*forcing* our *interpretation on their consciences!* When we say to them we think you mistaken,—do we treat them *precisely* as though they *avowedly contradicted* Christ and his Apostles? Whoever is capable of believing this, is beyond the reach of the conviction of evidence. There is not a church in the

* Vide Con. et Decret. Concil. Trident. sessio iv. Mannock's Poor Man's Controversy, p. 17—22. Printed *permissu superiorum*.

world where any species of order of any kind is preserved, that may not be accused in the same way.

Similar to this is the charge of "*imposing their own sense of scripture on their brethren* (p. 133.). It seems then, we must either bear the reproach of "imposing" our "own sense of scripture" upon others, or we must have Mr. Hall's "sense of scripture" "*imposed*" *upon us*. We are not to act for ourselves while we leave others the full liberty of doing the same, without being charged with the tyrannical assumption of popery!

"Both the church of Rome, and the church of England," says Mr. Hall, "have *devised terms of communion of their own*, and rendered it necessary for the members to comply with innumerable things besides those which Christ has enjoined as requisite to salvation. The *lawfulness* and *propriety* of doing so, is the *palmarium argumentum*, the main pillar and support of strict communion"! (p. 135.) This is a new charge. Leaving the churches of England and Rome to answer for themselves, WE, who plead that baptism is requisite to communion, are charged with maintaining the *lawfulness* and *propriety* of *devising terms of communion of our own*. If so, it will be no difficult matter to find those who will avow the principle. We do not presume to know the extent of Mr. Hall's information, but as far as our own observation has reached, we can safely affirm, that we never met with a single instance in which any man, either in writing or conversation, acknowledged the "*lawfulness and propriety*" of "*devising terms of communion*", to be "the main pillar and support of strict communion." In the present controversy such a principle was never stated, nor has any thing been adduced, which was intended to sanction that idea.

That this is the main pillar of our argument is so far from being true, that it is the OPPOSITE PRINCIPLE which we consider as our support. That baptism *was "devised"* by the Lord himself—*was* a term of communion—and has been so regarded by nearly all the christian churches in the world, and throughout all ages, Mr. Hall has been compelled to allow. Because it was a term of *Christ's* devising, we maintain that we have no right to alter it; we therefore boldly retort the charge, and assert that it is *Mr. Hall* who contends for the "lawfulness and propriety" of "devising terms of communion" unknown to the church in its purest ages; and if he fails to *prove his right* to make new terms, his cause is ruined. Could we conceive that we were justified in devising terms of "our own," we might be tempted to listen to what he has alleged. Yet even then we should pause, and inquire whether the plan formed by infinite wisdom, was not more likely to answer the ends of our great lawgiver, than any of our *devisings.* We remember it is written, "there are many devices in a man's heart, but the counsel of the Lord that shall stand. *Prov.* xix. 21. We say in the words of DR. OWEN, "Herein lies the *safety* of all believers and of all churches; namely to keep themselves precisely to the first complete revelation of divine truth in the word of God, let men *pretend* what they will, and *bluster* while they please; in an adherence to this principle we are safe; and if we depart from it, we shall be hurried and carried about through immeasurable uncertainties into ruin."*

Farther, "the church of England and the church of Rome", who are accused of having "devised terms of communion of their own," have also "rendered it necessary for the members to comply with *innumerable things* besides those which Christ has enjoined as requisite to salvation." If Mr. Hall means that these things were "enjoined" by Christ, but were not "enjoined as requisite to salvation," we ask for a list of them, that we may compare them with the present subject of debate, and see whether the authority

---

* Expos. on the Hebrews, abridged by Dr. Williams, vol. iv. p. 401.

which "enjoined" one precept, will not elucidate the regard that is due to another. If he means that these "innumerable things" were *not* "enjoined" by Christ; then we reply, there is a great difference between making those things "terms of communion" which Christ *never* "enjoined," and making that rite " a term" which *Christ* " devised," which *Christ* " enjoined," which once *was* a term of communion, and which Mr. Hall confesses is still in force, and ought to be "*restricted to believers,*" (*Reply, p.* 132.)

We ask, then, when that term which *Christ* " devised," became a term which *we* " devised?" Our author ought to shew, that Jesus Christ abrogated the terms which *he* himself appointed, and that then *we* devised the same terms, and enforced them on the ground of " the lawfulness and propriety" of devising terms of our own! If he fails in this attempt his charge is unsupported.

According to his representation, preserving an ordinance of Christ in its primitive situation, is "*devising*" *terms of our own:* and following the example of the church in its purest days in our regard to an institution which the Lord " enjoined," is put on the same ground with an adherence to "innumerable things which he never enjoined! But a farther exposure of so unfounded a statement, will probably be deemed needless. Every sober, reflecting mind will instantly see that the question is not—whether we *have*, or have not a *right* to devise terms of communion of our own—but whether the terms which Jesus Christ devised do not still continue in force. A considerable part of Mr. Hall's reasoning depends on the *assumption*, that we ought not to require obedience to a precept of Christ, as a term of communion, unless such obedience be requisite to salvation. So that on this plan, though the church is necessarily a visible body, and therefore requires visible institutions, yet we are not bound by those precepts which were given for the regulation of the church, unless it can be proved that they are requisite to salvation. Hence it follows that the directions of the Gospel are attended with so little authority, that a number of christians united as a church, have no right to say, these are the ordinances of the Lord, and therefore we ought to keep them as they were delivered to us. If, however, Mr. Hall should succeed in establishing his assumption, it will be difficult to say what innovation may not be established: for there is more evidence that the primitive churches were composed of members who were baptised, than there is of any other circumstance respecting their visible form and constitution: and if it is not needful for us in this instance to follow their example, and adopt their interpretation of the direction of their Lord, a similar train of argument will prove that we may divest ourselves of all regard to their authority in any thing else.

Towards the close of the chapter, our author has thought fit to resort to violent representations—to repeat the comparison of our system with the *opus operatum* of Popery—and to charge us with "faithfully" copying the "*arrogance*" of the Catholic church. Whatever his design may be in holding up his opponents in these dark colours, it ought to be remembered that if there is any truth in his statement, it equally applies to nearly the whole protestant church of every name and denomination. One of these attacks has been noticed already, and we promise to examine the rest, when it is shewn that *hard words* and *hard arguments* are the same things.

CHAPTER VII.

THE PÆDOBAPTISTS NECESSARILY PARTIES IN THE PRESENT CONTROVERSY.

MUCH offence has been taken with our former treatise, because it was there stated that *Pædobaptists* were parties in this controversy, and because some observations were made relative to the view which they would probably take of their situation were they admitted members of a Baptist church. Mr. Hall begins by descanting on the "majesty of truth," and the evils of falsehood, and corrupt suffrages: but after what we have been compelled to notice, it is rather surprising that he should say, "he who wishes to enlighten the human mind, will disdain to appeal to its prejudices, and will rather hazard the rejection of his opinion, than press them as a necessary corollary from *misconceptions and mistakes*"! (*p.* 136.)—Our author's intention in these remarks is, however, sufficiently manifest.

He repeats what he had asserted before, that Pædobaptists are not parties, and that it only interests them in the case of those who may be desirous of communing with us. (*p.* 137.) But this is a very partial view of the subject; and had not Mr. Hall shewn how completely he could overlook the bearings of the inquiry, we should have been surprised at his observations.

It is manifest that by far the majority of the Pædobaptist churches were founded on the acknowledgment of various principles—one of which was, that baptism was requisite to communion. Some evidence of this position was presented to the reader's notice in 'Baptism a term of Communion'; more might be adduced were it needful. Pædobaptists who possess only a moderate share of acquaintance with their own history, *know* that it is fact; and whether they do, or do not agree with their venerable predecessors, they will not deny that it has been the general opinion in their churches, that those who were admitted to communion ought *first* to be baptised. On this ground we said that they were parties; we repeat the assertion. All those who continue to maintain the sentiments which have been hitherto generally believed among them, will allow that the principle laid down in the former treatise was common to them as well as to us, that baptism was a " visible evidence of connection with the christian church." If they declare themselves converts to Mr. Hall's system, and assert that baptism is *not* a term of communion, they will still be parties; they will not only oppose *us*, but will become parties against us; and by deviating from the body of their predecessors, they must then set themselves against *their* arguments; they must place what they have hitherto held to be an institution of Christ on a new footing; they will, with Mr. Hall, practically lower the importance of what they have esteemed the rite of baptism, and prepare the way for its neglect; and they will, with him, endeavour to produce a REVOLUTION in the christian world of *an unexampled nature*. These consequences are so obvious, that they are not to be put down by the ridicule which Mr. Hall attempts to throw upon them.

Endeavouring to view the subject on all sides, on the ground hitherto acknowledged by both parties, we marked the natural and necessary consequences of Mr. Hall's system. In doing this, no candid Pædobaptist would mistake us, or think us surrendering our sentiments. It pleases Mr. Hall to say, " we should suppose him as tremblingly alive to the consistency of Pædobaptists, as Eli to the preservation of the ark. He adjures them by every thing they deem sacred not to forsake *him* in the conflict, reminding them that if they do so, they must abandon a multitude of positions which they have been accustomed to maintain against the Baptists (that is against himself), and be compelled to relinquish the field. He therefore exhorts them to be faithful unto death in the defence of error, and to take care that no arts, blandishments, or artifices, seduce them to concessions which would embarrass them in their warfare, and render the cause of infant baptism less tenable." (*p.* 138, 139.) Let the reader observe, here is no reference—no quotation—nothing but what Mr. Hall thinks fit to say, and to colour as he pleases. We ask, however, for no other indulgence, than that any reader of common sense and common candour would compare what our author has said with any paragraph we ever wrote, and then draw his own inference. What we said concerning the Pædobaptists occurs principally in two parts of our former treatise, and the end in view in each part was distinct. In the first, from p. 21—24, our object was to illustrate and apply a principle common both to Baptists and Pædobaptists;—a principle which Mr. Hall has thought proper entirely to overlook. In the second reference to the Pædobaptists, our object was to call their attention to the views which they ought to take of their own conduct if they sought communion with Baptists, and to the difficulties which they must encounter in justifying their own procedure, if they were thoroughly convinced that their own sentiments were right. This part of the discussion was in reply to the charge of bigotry which they urged against us, and was intended to shew, that unless they give up those views of baptism which hitherto they have generally retained (some of which are common to both parties, and some peculiar to themselves) it would be difficult for them to prove their consistency. (*Baptism a term of Com. p.* 114—118.)

In opposition to those observations, Mr. Hall gives us

the passage already quoted; which was obviously intended to make an impression so different from the fair interpretation of what we did say, that the mildest term that we can apply to it is, that it is *altogether a misrepresentation*.

His defence of what he has asserted is in the same style of accuracy: he culls an expression here, and another there, without any regard to the design of the author, or the object of his reasoning; and then gives us two pretended quotations, from p. 22 and 23 of Baptism a term of Communion, which are not copied with accuracy for two lines together.

Among other misrepresentations, there is one of a singular kind. Mr. Hall quotes one word, "degrading": he then connects it with an expression from *the succeeding paragraph*, which relates to a *different view* of the subject; there he finds it said—" that a Pædobaptist who refuses to commune with Baptists, because in so doing he tacitly allows himself to be considered as not so complete a disciple of Jesus as he thinks he is, acts a part which is justifiable and dignified." Part of this passage suits Mr. Hall's purpose: he connects "degrading"—with—" he is not so complete a disciple of Jesus as he thinks he is"; and then he tells us that "the amount of this reasoning is, that whenever a christian perceives that his brother entertains a less favourable opinion of his conduct *in any particular, than he himself does*, he is bound to renounce his communion; because in every such instance he must be considered as not so complete a disciple as *he* thinks he is, and to allow himself to be so considered is a meanness." (*Reply, p.* 142.) Not content with this, he adds, "and from hence another consequence infallibly results, that no two christians ought to continue in communion, between whom there subsists the smallest diversity of judgment respecting any point of practical religion; for since each of them, supposing them sincere, must believe his own practice more agreeable to the will of Christ than his brother's, that brother must be aware that he is considered as not so complete a disciple as he judges himself to be, to which it seems it is *degrading* to submit." (*p.* 143.) This recurs again in another form, and is represented as "a fine engine, truly, for dissolving every christian society into atoms:" (*p.* 144)—and repeating the expression that in "so doing he allows himself to be considered as not so complete a disciple as he thinks he is," Mr. Hall asserts in the next paragraph, that if this is a sufficient reason for a Pædobaptist's refusing to join with us, the consequence which he has deduced will follow. (*Reply, p.* 144.)

As Mr. Hall imagines he has got hold of a general principle, which he can apply against us, what he has urged may be thought by some, to require consideration. The paragraph from which he has selected a short member of one sentence, appears to us a sufficient refutation of his inference. In the first part, it is said, "let them [the Pædobaptists] consider whether" their joining with Baptists is not acting in a manner altogether inconsistent with *their views* of the law of Christ. They agree to be received, in the character of persons who have *not fulfilled* the will of their Lord, in the very point in which they believe they *have fulfilled it.*" &c. (*p.* 115.) To *this* sentence the expression refers which Mr. Hall repeats, that the Pædobaptist allows himself " to be considered as not so complete a disciple as he thinks he is," and by *this* sentence its propriety is to be tried. Here the inquiry related to *baptism* as a positive ordinance, which, by the supposition, the Pædobaptist believed he had obeyed; the importance of which he was also, in this view of the subject, supposed to maintain, according to the opinion which has usually been supported among Pædobaptists. On this ground the difficulty was put with fairness. It involved one inquiry, and, properly speaking, it involved no more; which was, what degree of regard a person ought to pay to those appointments which related to a *visible* connection with the christian body, and by which the *visible* church was intended to be separated from the world. Whoever thought the visible ordinances of the Lord were of importance, would necessarily feel reluctant in adopting any measure from which it must be inferred that he thought one of them of little consequence. A Pædobaptist (it was contended) was placed in this situation when he solicited admission among those whom he knew considered him to be unbaptised. He must form a slight opinion of the ordinance of baptism on the plan which he himself thought right, or he would not agree to be received as an *unbaptised* person. If he adopted the broad ground, that baptism is not necessary to communion, it was observed, that a fresh train of consequences followed;—these also were traced under a separate head, and urged on the Pædobaptist for his consideration *on his own principles.*

If any sober, intelligent man on either side of the question, will shew that we have *unfairly* stated the case between us and the Pædobaptists, or *unfairly* pressed on them the difficulties which arise from their own system, the subject shall be reviewed. But we do not think it necessary to lengthen the discussion by defending our statement, since Mr. Hall has done nothing more than avoid the argument, and torture expressions to a meaning which they did not convey.

If in the same spirit, an interpretation was given of many passages in the apostolic epistles, such as, "Now, I beseech you brethren, by the name of our Lord Jesus Christ, that ye all speak the *same thing*, and that there be *no divisions* among you; but that ye be *perfectly joined together* in the *same mind* and the *same judgment*," (1 *Cor.* i. 10) with other texts of similar import, nothing would be easier than to draw a train of ridiculous consequences from them, and then to add our author's flourish, "a fine engine truly, for dissolving every society into atoms, and for rendering the church of Christ the most proud, turbulent, and contentious of all human associations"! (*p.* 144.)

He pretends to make out *a contradiction* between two passages which occur in Baptism a term of Communion; in one of which we had said that the Pædobaptists "sacrificed *no principle*"; and in the other, that if their conduct was "connected with a *sacrifice of principle,* they will confess that it is indefensible." That we used these words is true; but they were not used in relation to the same, but to different things. It suits Mr. Hall's purpose at certain times to talk about *logic*: surely he must know, that it is a rule in logic, that to make *a contradiction*, it is necessary to assert that a proposition is true and false at the *same time*, in the *same sense*, and in the *same respect*.

CHAPTER VIII.

THE SCRIPTURE INJUNCTION RESPECTING FOR-
BEARANCE EXAMINED.

We are now arrived at that part of the discussion which relates to the scriptural directions respecting forbearance, particularly those which are found in the epistle to the Romans, ch. xiv; the principles on which that chapter is explained and applied in 'Baptism a term of Communion,' Mr. Hall shews he dislikes, but whether he is successful in his attempts to disprove them, and to establish his own, we will now examine.

A singular concession occurs towards the end of his seventh chapter, which materially affects his whole argument: he acknowledges, that "whatever is affirmed in any part of it [the New Testament], respecting the privilege of primitive believers, was asserted primarily of such *only* as were *baptised,* because there were *no others originally in the church:* all the reciprocal duties of christians were in the first instance enjoined on these; among which we find precepts enforcing without a shadow of limitation, the duty of cultivating christian fellowship." (*p.* 184.)

It seems then, that it cannot be concealed that the exhortation to receive those who were weak in the faith, was not to receive the *unbaptised,* as Mr. Hall would have *us* do; but to receive those who were already baptised, for "there were *no others originally in the church."* So that the exhortation was not, *receive into the church* those who were not then admitted; for the persons whom the Roman believers were exhorted to receive, were, according to our author's own confession, *in* the church. The question at that time was not,—how ought persons to enter the church according to the directions of the Lord?—but how should we treat those who *had entered* it in the way which the Lord required? Nor will any one doubt that such persons, though weak in the faith, should be the objects of great forbearance. But when this is granted, to all the extent that the New Testament requires, we are as far from Mr. Hall's conclusion as ever.

There is then, on his own concession, no similarity in *circumstances* between the Jewish converts who were "weak in faith" in the days of the Apostles, and those who at the present time are *unbaptised*. Let us next inquire, whether the *principle* of the exhortation to receive *Jewish converts* at that time, will justify us in receiving to communion the *unbaptised* now. If the *ground* of the Apostle's exhortation is, receive these weak brethren, although they neglect an institution which Christ delivered, and which was designed to be universally observed in his church; and let a desire to do them good and increase christian communion, induce you to give up in their favour what you believe was an appointment of the Lord;—then we admit that the principle of mixed communion is established. But if the practices and sentiments of the Jewish weak brethren, which the Apostle exhorted the Gentile christians to tolerate, did *not* set aside any command of Jesus Christ, but arose merely from their remaining attachment to abrogated rites, or to refinements on the law of Moses, which had never been divine appointments; then we contend that the case before the Apostles and the case of the *unbaptised* in any subsequent age, are so different in their *nature*, that the argument and exhortation of the Apostle, in Romans ch. xiv, cannot apply to both; and that Mr. Hall must obtain evidence from some other quarter if ever he establishes his point.

In Baptism a term of Communion we stated our view

of the debate between the Gentile and Jewish christians, and the principle on which the Apostle grounded his exhortation to forbearance: we then shewed that this *principle* did not apply to the cause now in hand. Mr. Hall thinks proper to call our "account" "egregiously partial"—"palpably designed to serve an hypothesis"—"a long and entangled dissertation" (*p.* 161): and if bestowing a few hard words upon it, is a sufficient reply, the deed is done. He then subjoins an "account" of his own: and afterwards he returns to the charge, and says, " still he will reply, that his error, [the error of the Jewish convert] is of a different kind from that of the Pædobaptists; he is guilty of no omission of a revealed duty; while they set aside a positive institute of christianity. It is by this distinction and this alone, that he attempts to evade the conclusion to which this example conducts us." Let the reader remark how Mr. Hall disposes of this distinction. "There is nothing however in reason or in scripture, from which we can infer, that to omit a branch of duty not understood, is less an object of forbearance, than to maintain the obligation of abrogated rites. Let him assign, if he is able, a single reason why it is less criminal to add to, than to take away from the law of Christ, to receive an obsolete economy than to mistake the meaning of a New Testament institute. How will he demonstrate willworship to be less offensive to God, than the involuntary neglect of a revealed precept?" (*p.* 165, 166.)

Doubtless these will be thought by some persons, entangling requisitions: the reply, however, is easy, scripture has shewn, and fact has demonstrated, that attention to the ritual observances of the Jewish law, was compatible with obeying all that Christ had commanded; but the scripture has given us *no precedent*, by which the church is authorised to receive those to communion, who oppose any precept of universal obligation which the Lord has enjoined.

A direct attack then follows: "the above distinction is not only unfounded in the nature of things; it is at variance with the reasoning of Paul on the subject. He enjoins the practice of forbearance on the ground of the *conscientiousness* of the parties concerned, on the assumption not only of their general sincerity, but of their being equally actuated in the very particulars in which they differed by an unfeigned respect to the authority of Christ; and as he urges the same consideration as the ground on which the toleration of both parties rested, it must have included a *something* which was binding on the conscience of each, whatever was his private judgment of the points in debate. The Jew was as much bound to tolerate the Gentile, as the Gentile the Jew." After quoting some verses from Rom. xiv. he adds, "now in the judgment of the Jew, still attached to the Mosaic rites, he who made no distinction of meats, or of days, must have been considered as violating, or neglecting, a precept still in force, or the injunction to refrain from judging him, would have been devoid of meaning. He must have consequently been regarded by him, in precisely the same light in which our Pædobaptist brethren are considered, that is, as violating, though not intentionally, a positive institute. Still St. Paul absolutely insists on the duty of forbearance," &c. (*p.* 166, 167.)

As there is in this passage a show of argument, we will examine it. Mr. Hall says, "the above *distinction* is not only unfounded in the nature of things; it is at variance with the reasoning of Paul on the subject." The reader will keep in mind that this "distinction," as stated by Mr. Hall was, that the error of the Jewish christian was of a "different kind from that of the Pædobaptists; *he* is guilty of no omission of a revealed duty: while *they* set aside a positive institute of christianity: and our author has asserted, that it is "by this distinction, and by this *alone*", that we have attempted "to evade the conclusion" which he derives from the example under consideration. "The above distinction" he tells us, "is—unfounded in the nature of things." Does Mr. Hall mean that the "nature of things" admits of no such distinction; or, that it is not supported by fact? Which ever be his meaning, he will not find it easy to prove either of these positions. But since he gives us what he thinks is Paul's "reasoning" on the subject, this is open to examination.

We are told that Paul "enjoins the practice of forbearance on the ground of the *conscientiousness* of the parties concerned, on the assumption not only of their general sincerity, but of their being equally actuated in the very particulars in which they differed, by an unfeigned respect to the authority of Christ." (*p.* 166.) That he enjoined forbearance, that he supposed both parties were *conscientious*, and that he wished to conciliate them on this ground is granted. But the peculiarities of each party were not binding on the other; and this was the reason why both were exhorted to follow the dictates of their own consciences. The Gentile had no right to require the Jew to adopt *his* law of liberty, for the Gospel did not command the Jew to change his food when he became a christian. So also, the Jew had no right to demand that the Gentile should conform to *his* habits; the Gospel had not required it; and the Apostles continually resisted the encroachments which the Jews wished to make on the liberty of the Gentiles, because they knew it was contrary to the will of God. Mr. Hall himself had informed us, that the "supreme legislator had repealed" the Mosaic dispensation; that in this chapter "St. Paul was testifying, the Lord Jesus had shewn him that nothing was unclean of itself;" and before this time "Peter had proclaimed the vision by which he was instructed, that the distinction of clean and unclean was abolished." (*p.* 164, 165.) It therefore necessarily followed, that as there was no rule by which either party could bind the other to adopt *his* practice, nothing remained but to leave his brother to obey the dictates of his own conscience; and if from general observation, they were satisfied with each other's integrity, they were then directed to practise mutual toleration. Now, if Mr. Hall can prove, that the principle on which the Apostle settled the difference between the Jewish and Gentile converts, applies to the case now before us; if he can prove that Baptists, Pædobaptists, and those who are for no baptism at all, have *the same authority from the Apostles*, for persevering in their respective opinions, that the Jews and Gentiles had for continuing in their different modes of living: that the question whether we are to use any baptism or none, as little concerns the Kingdom of God, as that of meat and drink, we will instantly grant, that it ought to take its place among those things for which there is no binding, universal rule, but which must be left to the decision of private feelings, of prejudice, of taste, or of inclination.

Our author adds, that since the Apostle " urges the same consideration as the ground on which the toleration of both parties rested, it must have included *a something* which was binding on the conscience of each, whatever was his private judgment of the points in debate." Suppose we admit this statement, that "*something*" was, that they had no right to require of their fellow christians a subjection to what *Christ* had not commanded; and in things which did not interfere with his commands, it was their duty to leave their brethren to act in the way most agreeable to their own feelings.

"The Jew was as much bound to tolerate the Gentile, as the Gentile the Jew." We grant he was, for he could not bring forward a law which required the Gentile to adopt the manners of a Jew, and therefore *must* leave him to the dictates of his conscience. " Now in the judgment of the Jew, still attached to the Mosaic rites, he who made no distinction of meats or of days, must have been considered as violating or neglecting a precept still in force, or *the injunction* to refrain from judging him, *would have been devoid of meaning.*" Not at all, the "injunction" was plain; it was, do not *condemn* the man you cannot *convict.* The *christian* church could not with consistency censure any of its members for not keeping the *Jewish law:* all that could be said concerning him was, "let every man be fully persuaded in his own mind."

The Apostle tells the Jew in a variety of ways through the whole of this chapter, that the Mosaic law was *not* in force;—that the Gentiles were *not* under obligation to submit to it;—that if *he* felt it binding on *his* conscience, he had no right, by the authority of Christ, to impose it on a Gentile believer;—that he had no business to judge another man's servant: "to his own master he standeth or falleth; yea, *he shall be holden up,* for God is able to make him stand." A gentle way of informing the Jew, that *he was altogether mistaken:* and though he had imagined that his zeal would promote the honour of the Lord, and that he was " actuated by an unfeigned respect for the authority of Christ," yet he had misunderstood the Gospel—and must not repeat his former arguments, for they were not founded on fact.

But, says Mr. Hall, the Gentile must consequently have been regarded by the Jew "*in precisely the same light* in which our Pædobaptist brethren are considered, that is, as violating, though not intentionally, a positive institute; still St. Paul absolutely insists on the duty of forbearance." (*p.* 167.) This is the point to which Mr. Hall wishes to bring the whole. The inference is, the Baptist is bound to tolerate the Pædobaptists, though their conduct in his esteem is a violation of a "positive institute," and the Apostle is quoted as authority for this practice. But when we examine what he has written, we find, that the Jew was exhorted to tolerate the Gentile, because he was told, that the "positive institute" which he imagined the Gentile had "violated," was not binding on the Gentile; for it was no part of the will of Christ that he should conform to the law of Moses, and therefore he ought to have the liberty of following the dictates of his own conscience. Now, we boldly ask, is the Baptist bound by similar authority to admit that *his* sentiment stands on the same footing—that it is no part of the will of Christ, but is only an attachment to an abrogated rite? Have the "Holy Ghost" and "the Apostles and Elders" as much sanctioned *Pædobaptism*, as they sanctioned the Gentile in his christian liberty respecting meat and drink? If they have, let it be proved, and we will yield the cause: for then the baptism of believers, and the Mosaic rites, may all be set aside together.

According to this comparison, the Pædobaptist is like the Gentile, who violated a precept which the Jew esteemed to be still in force, and the Baptist, like the Jew, is "*weak in the faith*", scrupulously attached to a needless institution, while in every point except his "*conscientiousness*", he is told that he is in an error! Of course the Pædobaptist occupies the place of the "*strong*", who is exhorted to tolerate his weak brother, and not bear hard upon him. A conclusion which some people will instantly admit, but how others will relish it, remains to be proved.

If we adopt the opposite hypothesis, and conceive the Jew to be the weak brother, and a representative of the Pædobaptists, we shall not succeed better in applying the principles of the chapter before us. It is true there is something in the first appearance of this plan of interpretation, which to a Baptist who is favourable to mixed communion, looks plausible, and he may be tempted to think it correct. He supposes that the Apostle is on his side with respect to baptism, and that he is directed to receive the Pædobaptists on the same ground that the Gentiles were to receive the Jewish converts, as *weak* brethren, who, it is true, were to be *tolerated*, but who were very much prejudiced, and very deficient in the extent and accuracy of their views. Reading the chapter with this idea, the Baptist observes that throughout the whole the Jew is plainly told that he is wrong, though the Apostle says, receive him: and he does not forget to make the proper application.

But examination soon dissipates this theory. The Jew did not attempt to come into the church without paying the required regard to the ordinances of the Gospel; he did not say, I have been initiated into the true religion by circumcision, I have frequently fulfilled the rites of baptism as required by the law; I therefore see no need of repeating any ceremony of initiation or profession, and I hope you will receive me, without pressing an attention to mere ceremonies, of the importance of which I am not convinced. No Pædobaptist, however, can come into a Baptist church except on terms precisely of this kind. He asks to be received, either on the ground of his Pædobaptism (which Mr. Hall himself tells us is "*a nullity*," and cannot be called baptism), or on that broad basis which would admit a person without baptism at all. He therefore stands in a very different situation from that of the Jewish converts, not only in its *circumstances*, but in its *principle*; for we have no evidence that any of the institutions of Jesus Christ were set aside, either for the purpose of receiving *them*, or *any other persons whatever*.

Farther, the practical exhortation which the Apostle gives (*ver.* 13, *&c. to the end*), proves that the ground of the Apostle's reasoning in this chapter cannot apply to the case in hand. He intreats the strong to give way to the prejudices of the weak, and so to conform their habits to the wishes of their erring brethren, as not to hurt their minds by eating that food which they might eat consistently with christian liberty. "It is good neither to eat flesh, nor to drink wine, nor any thing whereby thy brother stumbleth, or is offended, or is made weak. Hast thou faith? have it to thyself before God." (*ver.* 21, 22.) Though you are right, yet in tenderness to others do not openly act upon your opinion. So also ch. xv. 1. "We then that are strong ought to bear the infirmities of the weak, and not to please ourselves." Hence, if we apply the principle to the case before us, neither party ought to administer what they believe is an ordinance of Christ, whenever it would hurt the minds of those who think it a departure from the primitive institute. An inference urged upon us from different quarters, but the direct tendency of which is to exclude one of the ordinances of Christ from his church.

If on Mr. Hall's interpretation of the Apostle's directions, we ought to receive a Pædobaptist as a *weak brother*, for the same reason that the Gentile is exhorted not to grieve his brother by his meat, but to walk charitably, the Baptist ought not to plead for that baptism which grieves his Pædobaptist brother; much less ought he to shock his feelings by attempting to practice it; and above all things, he ought not to administer it to any friend or relation of the Pædobaptist, for this would be a want of charity in the extreme; but on the old plea, the ordinance should be *prudently shunned*, and that we may follow the things that make for peace, we are quietly to sacrifice an institution of Jesus Christ!

On this part of the subject we shall only add one remark more. *Mr. Hall* says with great positivity—"it is not, *be it remembered*, by a peremptory decision of the controversy, or by assigning the victory to one in preference to the other, that the Apostle attempts to effect a reconciliation." (*p.* 168.) But PAUL says, "I KNOW, *and am* PERSUADED *by the* LORD JESUS, *that there is nothing unclean of itself.*" (*Rom.* xiv. 14.) Unless the Jewish convert wanted common sense, he must see that the "decision of the controversy" *was given against him;* and though the Apostle was tender to his feelings, gave way to his scruples, and acknowledged that to him who "*esteemeth any thing to be unclean, to him it is unclean*", yet he clearly intended the Jew to understand that the precept which he imagined the Gentile "violated", had no authority. Hence, in whatever view this chapter is considered, the most that can be inferred from it is, that christians should tolerate each other in things which do not interfere with the precepts and institutions of Jesus Christ.

Hitherto we have proceeded on Mr. Hall's view of the subject, and have offered nothing in defence of our own interpretation. A few short observations in its justification will not, we hope be deemed improper.

It is manifest that the Jewish converts did obey the Mosaic ceremonies, and probably considered themselves under obligation to walk orderly and keep the law. (*Acts* xxi. 21—24.) In Rom. ch. xiv. the question which had been agitated, was not whether the weak brother should eat that which the law of Moses denominated *unclean*; but whether he might eat animal food at all. Two causes might give rise to this difficulty; a sect of the Jews called the Essenes refrained from animal food altogether, and if any of them were converted to christianity, they would probably be under the influence of their former prejudices, at least for a time. Some very learned men have thought that these were referred to by the Apostle in this chapter. Besides, we *know* that conscientious Jews *did* refrain from animal food *at Rome* about this time, and that their doing so was considered by their brethren as acting consistently with their profession as Jews.* The probable reason of which was on account of the numerous idolatries practised in that city; so that they were afraid of being polluted by eating meat which had been offered to idols, or which had not been prepared for their use, and declared to be *clean*

* An instance of this kind occurs in the Life of *Josephus*, the Jewish Historian.

by their own countrymen. Such scruples might also extend to Gentile christians, who might be afraid of the pollution of idols; and in proportion to their own tenderness of mind, would be hurt at seeing others do what they thought wrong. The eighth and tenth chapters of the first epistle to the Corinthians are devoted to this subject; and whosoever carefully and candidly considers the instructions which the Apostle gave to the christians at Corinth, can scarcely help seeing a great similarity to those which he gave to his brethren at Rome, and will acknowledge that the clear and important distinctions which he made in writing to the Corinthians, assist us in comprehending his directions to the Romans; and that there was a great resemblance between the cases described in these epistles. These general observations might be supported by a considerable body of proof, were it needful; and which would also confirm the interpretation of Rom. xiv. in Baptism a term of Communion. But since it is no part of our desire needlessly to lengthen the present controversy, we shall leave the reader to consider the evidence laid before him, and to form his own opinion; only reminding him, that Mr. Hall condemned what he did not like, after a very summary process, but did not disprove it.

However, to make assurance doubly sure, he does not content himself with the answer he had already given, but adds, "we accept Mr. Kinghorn's challenge, and engage to produce an instance of men's being tolerated in the primitive church, who neglected an express command of Christ, and that of the highest moment." (*p.* 171.) As he quotes no page, and copies no words that we have used, he leaves the reader to guess at what he refers. But, we suppose he had in his eye, an observation in Baptism a term of Communion, p. 50, where it is said, "I believe the truth is, that *there is not a case on record, in which forbearance and toleration were urged as reasons for setting aside* ANY *divine institute, which at the time was in force."* Now what is Mr. Hall's "instance"? It is the *Apostles!* He says, "it will not be denied that he [Christ] directed them to go forth *immediately* after the descent of the Spirit, to preach the Gospel to every creature." (*p.*171.) Because they did not proceed *immediately,* Mr. Hall attempts to justify his own theory by a bold crimination of inspired Apostles! It does not, however, appear that they neglected the dictates of their divine master. They were to *begin at Jerusalem.* (*Luke* xxiv. 47.) The Lord said unto them just before his ascension, "ye shall receive power after that the Holy Ghost is come upon you, and ye shall be witnesses unto me, both in Jerusalem, and in all Judea, and in Samaria, and unto the uttermost parts of the earth." (*Acts* i. 8.) A large field was to be the scene of their labours, *before* they went to the Gentile nations; and they occupied every part in its order. Nor did Peter resist the command given him to go with the messengers of Cornelius, and open the door of faith unto the Gentiles, as soon as he understood that this was the will of God. But Mr. Hall's inaccuracy in saying that the Apostles were directed to go forth to the heathen *immediately,* is not his only failure in the instance he professes to bring forward. He does not fulfil the terms of the requisition. Is it *upon record* that they endeavoured to *set aside* the command to preach the Gospel to the Gentiles, and that *toleration and forbearance* were either urged *by* them, or urged in their defence, as reasons why they might evade that precept? If not, Mr. Hall's instance proves nothing: it does not agree with the conditions of the case required.

Not content with one "instance" destitute of proof, he gives us another, "in which Mr. Kinghorn himself will be found to approve of the toleration of such as have habitually neglected a positive command" (*p.* 173); which is, that Dr. Gill and Mr. Brine influenced many of our denomination to believe that "it was improper to urge sinners to repentance, or to enjoin upon them the duty of believing on the Lord Jesus Christ." So that, these "eminent persons, in declining to perform what our Lord commanded his Apostles, neglected or broke a divine precept." The inference is, that if we do not mean to "pass a sentence of *excommunication*" on DR. GILL, MR. BRINE, and those whom Mr. Hall calls our "precursors in this controversy," we "must acknowledge that the right of toleration extends to such as neglect or violate a revealed precept." (*p.* 174.) He then adds, "it is unnecessary to remind the reader of the *magnitude* of the error in question, which would at once have annihilated the apostolic commission, by rendering it impossible to preach the Gospel to *any creature*, since there were in the Gentile world, none to whom on this principle it could be addressed." (*p.* 174.)

Without noticing the singular proposal to excommunicate the *dead*, let us inquire whether, if they were now alive, they would deserve excommunication. *Dr. Gill* distinctly states, that the Apostles were commanded to go—"not only into Judea—not only into the Roman Empire—but into every known and habitable part of the whole universe, to all the nations of the world under heaven :—and besides, this commission not only included the Apostles, but reaches to all Ministers of the Gospel in succeeding ages, to the end of the world." After some criticism on the word 'creatures,' in which he shows that the Jews by that term frequently meant the heathen, he proceeds,—"Now to these Christ would have the Gospel preached, as well as to the Jews; even *to all*, without any distinction of people, Jews and Gentiles, Barbarians, Scythians, bond and free, male and female, rich and poor, greater or lesser sinners, even *to all mankind.*"—(*See his Exposition on Mark* xvi. 15.) So also on *Matt.* xxviii. 19, he says, "*teach all nations*, Jews and Gentiles, first the one and then the other, the doctrines of the Gospel, and the ordinances of it; whatever they had learned from Christ, or were ordered by him."

A part of Mr. Hall's charge against *Dr. Gill* and *Mr. Brine* is, that "it was *improper* to urge sinners to *repentance.*" *Dr. Gill* certainly was not of this opinion. He says, "men of all nations, Jews and Gentiles, are the subjects of repentance; for all are under sin, under the power of it, involved in the guilt of it, and liable to punishment for it; and God *hath commanded all men every where to repent.* During the time of John the Baptist, and of our Lord's being upon earth, the doctrine of repentance was only preached to the Jews; but after the resurrection of Christ, he gave his Apostles an *instruction* and *order*, that repentance and remission of sins should be preached in his name among all nations, beginning at Jerusalem; in consequence of which the Apostles first *exhorted* the Jews, and then the Gentiles *to repent*, and particularly the Apostle Paul testified both to the Jews and also to the Greeks, repentance towards God, as well as faith towards our Lord Jesus Christ." (*Body of Div.* vol. iii. book 1. ch. 25. p. 33, 34. *Oct. ed.*) It would be easy to add farther testimonies, but these are sufficient. Let then the candid reader judge, whether there be any ground for *excommunicating* DR. GILL, on the charge of annihilating "the apostolic commission, by rendering it impossible to preach the Gospel to *any creature*"? The speculations of *Dr. Gill* and *Mr. Brine*, on the nature of what they termed *special faith*, formed the great peculiarity of their sentiments; for this they considered as an effect of the mediation of Christ, and the duty of those only who received "an internal revelation of Christ," which they called also "a supernatural revelation."* But they both declared that it was the duty of men to *give credit to any revelation* which God had made, or should think fit to

---

* *Brine's* Refutation of Arminian Principles, p. 6. 19.

make unto them at any time: and whether they did or did not reason correctly on the nature of faith, they did *not* set aside the divine institute, that the Gospel should be preached unto all men, as the means of bringing sinners to God; but acknowledged, that "every truth should be preached—none concealed;—and no duty omitted." So that when we examine Mr. Hall's second "instance" it does not comply with the terms of the requisition, better than the former.

In the preceding observations, we have taken no notice of one of Mr. Hall's violent misrepresentations, which is the basis of many animadversions. In Baptism a term of Communion it was pleaded, that the Apostle's argument applied equally, whether we considered Jews, or Gentiles as the parties received: and it is added, "but then he [God] receives them on their believing and obeying his Gospel; and it is not stated, that he receives them notwithstanding they disobey one of its precepts. Yet unless this be proved, the cause of mixed communion is not promoted." (*p.* 45. 2*d ed*,) On this passage, Mr. Hall thinks proper to say, "we have here an explicit avowal that he considers none besides the Baptists as received of Christ, in the sense the Apostle intends, accompanied with a concession that to prove they were, would furnish an irrefragable argument for our practice." (*p.* 153, 154.) So also in *p.* 207,—" he professes to imitate the conduct of the Supreme Legislator, whom *he affirms*, not to have received the unbaptised into the gospel dispensation." Had we not seen instances of a similar kind, such statements would have excited surprise. It is easy to perceive, that if it could be proved that God had received either party into his visible church without baptism, or while they were opposing any universal precept which he had promulgated, Mr. Hall's argument for receiving the unbaptised would have been established by the precedent which was furnished by the divine conduct: but as this was not the fact, the cases were not parallel. In examining how the argument then stood, nothing more was necessary, than to satisfy a fair inquirer, that the Gentiles were not received into the church on the principle for which Mr. Hall pleaded for admitting the unbaptised: the inference therefore followed, that his cause could not be promoted by such reasoning. But here he takes occasion to talk about an "explicit avowal," where nothing was avowed that agrees with his representation.

Whoever examines the New Testament on this subject, will see, that God testified by the miracles he wrought, that the Gentiles could be received into the full enjoyment of the blessings of the Gospel; and when the Apostle Peter saw that on the Gentiles was poured out the gift of the Holy Ghost, he commanded them to be baptised. *Then* they would be considered as received into the church, but not before. Now if the reception of the Gentiles into the christian church on their being baptised, is authority for our receiving into the church the *unbaptised*, the argument is finished. But how is Mr. Hall to prove this position?

He would persuade us that persons *unbaptised*, applying for church-membership with Baptists, are in the same situation with the believing Gentiles when they *were baptised:* but it is manifest that the cases are dissimilar, and every attempt to make them alike utterly fails. It is to no purpose that, under the pretence of "sifting the matter to the bottom," he should attempt by wire-drawing and misrepresentation, to build up his cause. Let him prove that the Gentiles refused to be baptised, or that they refused to comply with any other positive, universal precept of Jesus Christ, and then we will allow, that whatever is the principle of the Apostle's reasoning, will apply in both cases. But since, for the best of all reasons, this is not done, we hold Mr. Hall's violent distortions of the argument very cheap: they may hurt himself,—they do not hurt our cause. But the truth is, that as the fourteenth chapter of the Romans is the great storehouse of argument for mixed communion, every thing which shows that the principles of the apostolic church and of modern innovation are not the same, must be disposed of, and if an answer cannot be found, it must be run down.

Mr. Hall requests the reader to advert to the "interminable discord and dissention with which *this principle* is replete. The principle is, that whenever one christian deems another to live in the neglect and violation of a positive command, however conscientious and sincere, he must renounce the communion of the party which he supposes erroneous." (*p.* 174, 175.) Let the reader observe that this principle which Mr. Hall adduces, is an inference of his own. He had been pressed to produce a case, if such a case was on record, in which forbearance and toleration were urged as reasons for setting aside *any* divine institute, which at the time was in force. His reply proclaims his inability to bring forward such an instance. We are then told that the "principle" which he thinks proper to draw from the fact urged against his reasonings, " is replete with interminable discord:" as if we were to be frightened from an attention to the directions of Christ, because Mr. Hall chooses to say, that pleading for the primitive order of the ordinances of the Gospel, is the way to produce dissention! To make his own cause look better, he enumerates various differences of sentiment respecting the " minuter details of christian discipline and worship": he acknowledges that they are cases difficult to settle ; and he says, " there are no questions involved in greater obscurity than these; none on which the evidence is less satisfactory, and which more elude the researches of the learned, or administer more aliment of dispute to the contentious." (*p.*175,176.) Such is his opinion of the systems which he himself brings forward. Now observe his inference: " however they may differ in other respects, they agree in this, that upon the principle we are attempting to expose, they furnish to such as adopt them, just *as reasonable a pretext* for separate communion, as the disagreement concerning baptism," &c. (*p.* 177.)

Here the appeal lies to the common sense of men: we pleaded for the regard that was due to *baptism* from the various arguments which we have before recited; Mr. Hall himself confessed that *our views* of the subject, as Baptists, have "all the advantage of *overwhelming evidence*" (*Pref. p.* xxiii.); but yet he would persuade us, that those persons whose opinions, according to his own statement, are *not* supported by satisfactory evidence, but are involved in the greatest obscurity, have as much reason for requiring that others should adopt their peculiarities, as we have for pleading from the commission of Christ, and the acknowledged, universal practice of the apostolic church, that baptism is requisite to a participation of the Lord's supper!

On this plan, the command of Christ respecting baptism, considered as a regulation for his church is USELESS; and the precept is now become merely an affair of private opinion! A consequence which meets us in every part of this discussion; and which, however unwilling some may be to acknowledge it, will at length be confessed to be the natural result of our author's reasoning.

CHAPTER IX.

Mr. Hall's argument for communing with pædobaptists, because they are part of the true church, examined.

That part of the discussion which next comes forward to notice is, in our view, deserving of very little attention: but were it wholly omitted, it might be thought that its arguments were unanswerable. Many things which are open to exception, we shall pass over, merely for the sake of brevity; others we shall leave to the decision of the reader, who, if he has read both sides, will be able to form his own opinion. Some few assertions of Mr. Hall must, however, be noticed, and some of the usual accompaniments of his work pointed out.

We shall say nothing concerning Mr. Hall's notions of 'the church'; we are not sure that we comprehend his theory, and would not, knowingly, draw an inference from false premises. In our apprehension he confounds things which are distinct; and uses a manner of expression which is open to exception. If any person who had read Baptism a term of Communion, should declare that we did not acknowledge that many who differed from us were *christians*, we should probably not attempt to convince him of the contrary; and as to Mr. Hall's inference about *schism*, we leave that to refute itself. *He* maintains *a schism*, and will only take those who come to *his terms*; and after he has said the worst things he can of us, we do no more. But passing this, let the reader observe the ground on which Mr. Hall justifies his own separation from other christians.

"Whenever we are invited to concur in practices which we esteem erroneous, or corrupt, our refusal to comply is justified by a principle the most obvious and the most urgent, the previous obligation of obeying God rather than man." *(p. 192.)* Again, "owing to a diversity of judgment, respecting the proper organization of churches, obstacles, at present invincible, may prevent their incorporation; and it is left to the conscience of each individual to determine, to which he will permanently unite himself. An enlightened christian will not hesitate for a moment, in *declining* to join with that society, *whatever be the piety of its individual members*, in which the terms of communion involve his concurrence in religious observances of whose lawfulness he entertains any doubt. Hence arises, in the present state of religion, an impassable barrier to the perfect intercommunity of christian societies." *(p.*193, 194.) It seems then, that there may be societies, composed of *individual members* of acknowledged *piety*,—persons whom our author would certainly consider to be parts of the *true church*, with whom an *enlightened christian* not only would not join, but would *not hesitate for a moment* in *declining* to join. The ground on which this *enlightened christian* would act so promptly, would be that the terms of communion involved his concurrence in religious observances of whose lawfulness, he entertained *a doubt.* So that in the absence of certainty, even *a doubt* on the propriety of his conduct would make him pause.

After having thus plainly conceded the principle on which we rested one part of our cause, Mr. Hall adds, "*but it is* NOT *upon this ground that my opponent objects to the practice for which we are contending*." If the reader refers to Baptism a term of Communion, he will find in *that chapter* which relates to the present part of the argument, a variety of passages which shew the ground on which it was placed, and he can then judge how far Mr. Hall is correct in his assertion.

"The friends of strict communion do not object to mixed communion, because the individual act of their communion with Pædobaptists would produce an immediate unpleasant effect on their worship; but because it would be the acknowledgment of *a principle* which they cannot admit; which is, that in forming a part of the church of Christ, there is no occasion to regard the term of christian profession which he himself has appointed; and thus the introduction of mixed communion, would itself immediately *alter the constitution of every church that adopts it.*" *(p.* 58.)

Again, "The Protestants, and Protestant Dissenters, *refuse* to unite with Roman Catholics, and the Establishment, because in so doing, they would sanction what they believe are corrupt appendages to the law of the Saviour. The strict Baptist *refuses* to admit those whom he considers as unbaptised, because in so doing he would sanction the omission of an express part of the law itself; though he grants the individual excellency of many men in all the churches from which he differs." *(p.* 64.)

Farther, "the objection of the strict Baptists to communion with them [the Pædobaptists] does not arise from suspicions attaching to their *christian character,* to which, they trust, they are always willing to render ample justice, but from the necessary consequence of such communion; as a practical deviation from what they believe was the *original constitution of the church.*" (*p.* 67, 68.)

Once more, the question is brought to this point,— "whether the admission of mixed communion does not *of itself* introduce into the church a system of action which is NOT a true interpretation of the rule given by the Lord, and NOT a copy of the precedents of the New Testament, NOR a just application of its maxims." *(p.* 76.)

All these passages are copied from one chapter; and that chapter in which the present part of the discussion is expressly examined. The reader can now judge for himself on *what ground* we object to the practice which Mr. Hall advocates. He can also judge how far the next assertion which our author makes is supported by *truth*, which is, that we rest our "refusal to communicate with members of other denominations, on the principle of their not being entitled to be *recognised as christians.*" *(p.* 194.)

The argument repeatedly urged, that communion with the unbaptised *altered the constitution* of the church of Christ, and introduced a line of conduct unknown in the purest ages, Mr. Hall has *never encountered.* If he imagines that we esteem either his silence, or the contempt with which he treats this part of the subject a sufficient refutation, he is mistaken. He says himself, "let the *smallest error imaginable* be so incorporated with the terms of communion, that an *explicit assent to it* is implied in that act; and he who discerns it to be an error, must, if he is conscientious, dissent, and establish a separate communion." *(p.* 211.) On his own ground, then, the question is, whether in communion with the *unbaptised* we do not give an "*explicit assent*" to the right of admitting them *in that character* into the church? On this basis our objection to mixed communion was founded, and pressed on the reader's attention, and we contended, that there was necessarily and explicitly implied in it the admission of an *unscriptural proposition.* But when the principle on which our argument rested was urged against Mr. Hall, he passed it by, and the reader is told that our objection to mixed communion is NOT placed on this ground!

Still it is said,—we are not invited to concur in those "*religious observances*" which we disapprove, and that fellowship with Pædobaptists is only a "transient act"; *(p.* 192.) but we reply, we understand our ground sufficiently not to be deceived by such expressions. We are "invited to concur," in an act the consequences of which would be *permanent;*—in the admission of a principle which we believe to be unscriptural, opponent to the authority of Christ, and subversive of one of his institutions. Were we to adopt it, we should instantly be told we had *altered* our terms of communion; and the charge would be just; we should then have introduced a "*new term*" which Christ did not make, which was unknown in the apostolic church; and we should sacrifice one of the ordinances of the Gospel, for the professed purpose of gaining a greater number of persons to attend with us to the other.

Whenever the question is asked, what are the terms of communion mentioned in the New Testament, we cannot give a scriptural answer if we leave out baptism. Many queries may be raised respecting the best manner of procedure in the admission of members into the church, which do not admit of a direct reply from the sacred volume; but which must be decided by the application of general principles to particular cases. But every child that reads the New Testament with attention is capable of perceiving, that in the apostolic age it was those who were baptised that were added to the number of the faithful, and treated as parts of the body. While we act on the same plan we are safe; for we require no more than Christ required; and unless Mr. Hall can prove that according to the directions of the Lord, a church can be formed without baptism, he labours in vain; for the facts of the New Testament are against him, and all his arguments for his favourite theory are of no force.

CHAPTER X.

THE CHARGE OF EXCLUDING, EXCOMMUNICATING, AND PUNISHING OTHER DENOMINATIONS, CONSIDERED.

IN this part of the inquiry our author adopts a violence of language and an excess of misrepresentation that cannot ultimately benefit his cause. The first thing that we shall notice is his criticism on the use of words. This he pretends is "humiliating"; perhaps it is so: we will examine it. He objects to our use of the word "exclusion." He says that we deny "the propriety of applying the term to *a bare refusal of admission.*" (*p.* 198.) We have then a definition by "our great Lexicographer" *Johnson*. Now if we were incorrect in the use of the word, our author was guilty of the same fault.—He asks, (*p.* 104,) "will they assert that St. Paul was prepared to *exclude* the members of the church of Corinth, against whose irregularities he so warmly protested?"—Again, (*p.* 109,) "he continued to exercise forbearance without the slightest intimation of an intention to *exclude* them." In both these instances Mr. Hall thinks fit to use the term precisely in the sense which we had given it.

Then comes another criticism relating to the word *excommunication*; which, we are told, is "synonymous with exclusion," and again we have "the highest authority" brought forward, with a note, "see *Johnson.*" To *Johnson* we have referred, and find the authority which he quotes for his definition of the term is a passage taken from the Ecclesiastical Polity of *Hooker*. We know that the theological sentiments of *Johnson* and *Hooker* were the same: and we are certain, from *Hooker's* own declarations, that in his view baptism was necessary to church membership. He says, "entered we are *not* into the visible church, before our admittance by the door of baptism." (*Eccl. Pol. book* ii. § 1.) He clearly would have agreed with us, that a person who was never *in* the church, could not be expelled *from* it. In his view, excommunication, supposed previous membership. At length Mr. Hall employs words, the meaning of which are not disputed, and intimates that we "withhold privileges and immunities from him *who is legally entitled to their possession.* (*p.* 201.) On this ground we meet him; if he can prove that the *unbaptised* are "*legally entitled*" to the privileges and immunities of the church, the argument will be finished, and we shall not think of replying: but till this is done, all his reasoning proceeds on mere assumption.

He talks about "*punishment*", but let him prove that we withhold from those who he confesses are unbaptised, what they can claim according to the New Testament. Let him prove from that volume that our Lord intended one of his institutions to vanish away;—that he designed to alter the terms of communion which he himself established; let him shew how the institution of baptism can continue in force, while it has lost its station in the church; and then, but not till then, will we alter our plan of procedure. We know that a clamour is raised against us about the excellence of the persons whom we refuse to admit into our churches. But we reply, our concern is with the directions of the New Testament. If the admission of members depended on our opinion of their piety, *exclusive* of any regard due to an institution which Christ placed at the door of his church, the case would be different; but Mr. Hall has not succeeded in shewing that *this* should be our guide, instead of the directions and examples of the sacred volume. Unfortunately for his system, *the rule exists;* and as we have stated before, according to our views of the rule which the Saviour had given, it was not WE that excluded the unbaptised, but the plain interpretation of the will of Christ (*See Bap. a term of Com. p.* 61); and our author himself tells us, that "the interpretation of a rule is, to him who adopts it, equally binding with the rule itself, because every one must act on his own responsibility". (*p.* 110.)

Mr. Hall attempted to confound the expulsion of the incestuous Corinthian with the rejection of a Pædobaptist; and asserted, that both amounted " to a declaration of the parties being *unworthy* to "communicate". In Baptism a term of Communion, it was answered, (*p.* 61.) that the cases were not similar: "in one case the party *is* declared unworthy from moral delinquency: in the other he is not declared *unworthy*, but only *unqualified*". We should have supposed this statement was sufficiently clear to answer the purpose for which it was brought. In the first instance the objection was of a moral kind; in the second no such objection was adduced, or supposed to exist; but the reason why the party was not received, was on the acknowledged ground that he was unbaptised, on which account, he was in our view "*unqualified*": and it was immediately added, "whether this be, or be not true, is to be settled by an appeal to the New Testament."

On the occasion of this plain passage, Mr. Hall thinks fit to play on the terms—moral delinquency—unworthy, qualified, and—unqualified, as if some proposition had been brought forward which was either unintelligible or absurd. After the explanation given above, which is scarcely more than re-stating what was said before, we leave the paragraph to the common sense of reasonable men. What Mr. Hall says concerning it we think "*unworthy*" any farther notice.

Enough has been said to prove that the question was justly stated in 'Baptism a term of Communion,' *p.* 65. It is there observed, that this part of the discussion rests on an answer to the inquiry, "whether an institution of

Christ is to be maintained, or is to be given up"? Mr. Hall quotes a few lines,—calls them an "evasion", and attempts a reply. (*p*. 212, 213.) In the paragraph which he had before him it is stated, that the question is NOT whether the Pædobaptists were chargeable with nothing more than a misconception of a positive institute; NOR, whether the members of a church have fully and properly considered the nature of the institute to which they have submitted, for our author does not rest his system on this basis; on the contrary, he asserts that they have *not submitted to it at all*. But to whatever extent *they* misconceive it, *he* gives it up; for though he may admit that it has a claim on a christian's attention in his individual capacity, yet the whole of his labour is an attempt to exclude the institution from the station in which it was placed by Jesus Christ. On his plan of reasoning, the church ought to receive not only those who venerate the institution though they misconceive it, but those also who *ridicule* and *oppose* it. Hence the tendency of his system, as far as it is received, *is*, and *will be*, to encourage the popular notion that baptism is a trifle which may either be regarded, or not. His works form an inclined plane, down which the minds of those who are disinclined to obey the injunctions of the New Testament, descend to a neglect of, at least, *one* of the ordinances of the Gospel, and quiet themselves in the assurance, that if they do not believe baptism requisite to communion, they ought to have all the privileges of the church without it. So that instead of calling on men to "search the scriptures," his system holds out a bribe to the mind to pay the subject no attention.

The manner in which our author finishes his observations on the quotation before him, deserves notice: "if they [the Pædobaptists] are chargeable with any thing more than a misconception, the matter of that charge must be deduced from their acting like upright men; *an accusation, which we hope for the honour of human nature, will proceed from none but strict Baptists.*" (*p.* 214.) The first part of this passage needs no reply, because the preceding observations shew that it is not to the point; for we have never supposed that those who differed from us were *not* "upright men";—we have uniformly proceeded on the opposite hypothesis. The second part is an indiscriminate and unjust censure on a large body, and deserves no regard except as a specimen of that temper with which Mr. Hall's work so much abounds.

CHAPTER XI.

Mixed communion unknown in the ancient church.

We now come to the state of opinion in the ancient church, which we are told may be distributed into three periods. The first includes the time during which, correct sentiments on the subject of baptism prevailed, and in which, our author informs us, "a punctual compliance with it was expected and enforced by the presidents of the christian societies." (*p.* 217.) This period is supposed to extend to the end of the second century, or the beginning of the third. The second period begins from that date and proceeds to the close of the fourth century, during which time the baptism of infants was introduced and gradually extended. The third period includes the long course of years from thence to the commencement of the Reformation. During the first of these periods, it is allowed there could be no mixed communion; but in the second, Mr. Hall contends, there must have been Baptists and Pædobaptists in the same society, unless it could be proved that the Baptists maintained a separate communion.

Here he takes his stand, and asserts, that "no sooner did a difference of opinion on the subject of baptism arise, than the system of *forbearance* recommended itself at once, to all who adhered to the sentiments of the modern Baptists throughout every part of the world; and that it is the opposite principle which has to contend with all the odium and suspicion attached to recent innovations." (*p.* 219, 220.) "Hence", he says, "the concurrent testimonies of the Fathers of the three or four first centuries, in proof of the necessity of baptism to church fellowship, are urged to no purpose whatever, unless it could be shewn that there was no mixed communion, no association of the advocates of adult, with the patrons of pædobaptism, known in those ages." (*p.* 221.)

This statement has, we grant, the merit of novelty. But it cannot escape the observation of the attentive reader, that our author brings forward a representation, which in words appears in favour of his system, but in fact was unknown to all antiquity. Did the Baptists of that period receive the Pædobaptists into their communion as persons *unbaptised?* Did they admit them, while they declared their baptism *invalid,* and a *nullity?* Did they plead for their reception on the ground of *forbearance?*—We never met with the slightest evidence that *they did:* nor with any one who imagined that such evidence exists. Before Mr. Hall's statement can be admitted to have any force, he ought to prove that those who were received into the church in their infancy, were considered by the other members of the christian community as persons *unbaptised.* Till this is done his cause is not advanced a single step, and the statement which we before made continues in its full strength, that his theory was unknown in antiquity, and is an invention of modern date.

Innovations are made by degrees: when infants were introduced, the original mode of baptism was continued; they were baptised on a profession of faith made by proxies, who answered the usual questions in their name, and who engaged that as they grew up they should believe. The infants who were baptised in the early ages, for some time after the introduction of the practice, appear to have been few; and the extravagant notions then entertained of the consequence of baptism, especially when received from administrators who were high in public estimation, and were supposed to have spiritual blessings to communicate, induced men in general to believe such baptism valid. But the case would have been materially different had those who were baptised in adult years formed that opinion of baptism received in infancy, which Baptists now form of pædobaptism.

In our former treatise Cyprian was referred to, in consequence of Mr. Hall's having turned the reader's attention to that celebrated Father. We stated our view of the difference of opinion in ancient and modern times, on the point in hand, which our author thinks proper to neglect; and we then brought the question to this issue, "did the ancient church ever admit those to the Lord's table who then were considered as unbaptised?" (*Baptism a term of Communion, p.* 153, 154.) It is acknowledged such persons were *not* admitted; but it is alleged Cyprian admitted *Baptists and Pædobaptists,* which, for the reasons already given, is nothing to the purpose.

Mr. Hall says, we forget the importance which Cyprian "attached to baptism as a *regenerating* ordinance." (*p.* 229.) "In ancient times the necessity of baptism as a qualification for communion, was avowedly founded on its supposed essential connection with salvation." (*p.* 235.) We know that Cyprian called baptism *regeneration;* but it is evident he did not mean by that term what we understand by it; in his view a person who *repented* and *believed* was *not* regenerated till he was baptised; certain spiritual blessings were then conveyed which were not given before; and the African Father thought, that these blessings could not be enjoyed unless the *one baptism* which he considered of so much consequence, was received in *that* part of the christian community which he asserted was *alone* the church of Christ. In baptism, he informs us, children were born to God, and the church is their mother. The Apostle Paul teaches us the sacrament of Unity, saying, there is one body, and one spirit, one hope of

your calling one Lord, one faith, one baptism, one God.—
The unity of the church subsisted by celestial sacraments.* We are aware that the term *sacrament* was often used in a wide sense, but however it be applied, in the first expression, baptism is at least *included* in the sacrament of unity; and in the second, it cannot be *excluded*. As in the estimation of Cyprian, baptism could only be obtained in the true church, so it was essential to the existence of that church; and nothing, in his view, could be more absurd or heretical, than to imagine that a church might be formed on Mr. Hall's plan without baptism, or that the unbaptised might communicate with those who were baptised under the notion of promoting *unity!* He supposed that whoever did not hold the *unity* of the church, did not maintain the *faith* of the church; for the one faith and one baptism of the church he considered as essential to its unity. That these notions were extended a great way too far, every one except a Roman Catholic will acknowledge; but all considerate men, who have no system to serve, will grant with equal freedom, that the excess to which they were carried, and the principles on which they were founded, are strong presumptions that such reasonings as those of Mr. Hall were altogether unknown.

Yet notwithstanding the length to which the African Father carried his theory, he granted that there were cases in which persons might be saved who died without the "regenerating ordinance" of baptism. He allowed that Catechumens who were slain before they were baptised, and the thief on the cross, were of this description. He went still farther; when some of his brother Bishops had admitted persons into their churches who had been baptised by Heretics, he did not venture to deny that *even these* would partake of divine mercy. He thought his brethren ought not to have admitted them; yet, though he

* Vide Epist. ad Jubian. ad Pomp. et, De Unit. Eccl. § 4, 5, &c.

strongly stated his own opinion, he did not prescribe it as a law which other ministers were bound to follow. (*Vide Epist. ad Jubian.* § 19, &c.)

But suppose we suffer Mr. Hall to explain Cyprian's expressions so as to suit his hypothesis, we shall still find the maxims of antiquity inflexible; for though there were some who differed from the African Father, and seemed more nearly to approach Mr. H.'s sentiments, by admitting that in some cases the baptism administered by Schismatics and Heretics might be valid, and by pleading for the admission of those whose baptism Cyprian disapproved, yet neither party thought of admitting persons *unbaptised*. Mr. Hall thinks he has obtained a general principle which suits his purpose, and he repeats his charge that we violate "more maxims of antiquity than any other sect upon record." (*p.* 246.) But what are "the maxims of antiquity"? Is there any one more ancient or more universal than this—that communicants at the Lord's supper should be baptised? "Among all the *absurdities* that ever were held," says Dr. Wall, "none ever maintained *that*, that any person should partake of the communion before he was baptised." (*Hist. of Inf. Bap. ed.* 2. *p.* 518.)

We go farther, we retort the charge; it is *Mr. Hall* who violates the "maxims of antiquity." How can he describe the unity of the church, in agreement with Cyprian's "maxims," without condemning his own? How can he shew that any of those "maxims" which declared baptism to be the sacrament of unity that kept the church in one body, can be applied to a church formed on *his* principles? How can he prove that the ancients anticipated a "new case" in which the *unity* of the church was to be promoted by holding *different opinions,* and those who had *one* baptism, and those who had *none*, were to become one body? How can he carry his theory into practice, except by opposing the whole primitive church? How then can his "maxims" and their's be the same?

He thinks proper to find fault with our quoting the *Donatists* as acting on our general principle. Their conduct proves all that it was brought to prove. Between them and the Catholic church, there was no difference of opinion on the general doctrines of the gospel; but they thought the procedure of the Catholics had destroyed the spirit of their religion, and invalidated the ordinances of their church. Hence the Donatists urged the necessity of baptising those who, entering into *their* views and feelings, desired to hold communion with *them*. This single circumstance clearly shews, that instead of acting on Mr. Hall's principle, they acted on a principle diametrically opposite: for when they believed the converts to their system to be deficient in nothing else, they still deemed it requisite to baptise them, before they became members of the Donatist church.

The discussion respecting the opinion and practice of the ancient church, lies in a narrow compass. Great fault is found with our view of the sentiments of Cyprian; but whether we were correct or not, neither Cyprian nor those who opposed him acted on the theory laid down by Mr. Hall; nor do we recollect an instance in which any person whose baptism was considered invalid, was ever admitted on our author's favourite argument derived from *forbearance*. That *we*, however, might not know of such an instance, nor be acquainted with any ancient writer who reasoned on his principles may not appear surprising; but what *we* never met with, *his* diligence and acuteness might have discovered. Yet no such writer has been produced; nor a single instance brought forward in proof that his theory was even *known;* much less that it was *adopted*. The presumption, then, is stronger than ever, that he can find no support in antiquity. Notwithstanding all his opposition, the result is—during the apostolic age, it is confessed, there *could be no* mixed communion; and, during the succeeding early ages, it is manifest, there *was none*.

CHAPTER XII.

Conclusion.

In bringing our own work to a termination, we are naturally led to observe how Mr. Hall finishes *his*. Near the beginning, and at the close of his last chapter, he talks about a *religion of love*; but whether the representations with which he concludes his Reply, either proceed from *love*, or are calculated to promote it, demands a doubt.

Our author says, " it has been frequently observed on this occasion, that every voluntary society possesses the power of determining on the qualifications of its members; and that for the same reason, every church is *authorised to enact such terms of admission as it shall see fit*." (*p.* 255.) Again, " when therefore from its analogy to other societies, it is inferred that it [the church] has an equal right to organise itself at its pleasure, nothing can be more fallacious." (*p.* 256.) But who asserted this? That a religious society, laying the word of God before them, must necessarily judge of a candidate's qualifications, and determine whether they do, or do not accord with the requisitions of the scriptures, is evident; for unless Mr. Hall can prove that we have *no rule*, the only course we can pursue is to judge according to our ability *by* the rule. But this is a totally different thing from saying, that "every church is authorised to enact such terms as it shall see fit,"—and, " to organise itself at its pleasure";—a proposition which we never laid down; a charge for which our author alone is accountable. We allow, to use his words, that " the church is a society instituted by heaven, it is the visible seat of that kingdom which God has set up, the laws by which it is governed are of his prescribing,' (*p.* 255) and for this reason we oppose Mr. Hall's system. To us it appears inconsistent with our obligation " exactly to conform to the mandates of revelation," (*p.* 256) to " organise" the church at *our* pleasure, and to " enact" that one of the ordinances which Christ has appointed, shall be removed from its place.

"The Baptists, Mr. Kinghorn informs us, consider themselves as holding to notice *one* neglected truth." The reference is, ' Baptism a term of Communion, *p.* 69." What does Mr. Hall infer from hence? " it is the *principle* thus distinctly avowed, to which we object—the *principle* of organising a church with a specific view to the propagation of some particular truth." (*p.* 257.) We grant that we did say, the Baptists " hold up to notice *one* neglected truth." Will Mr. Hall deny either that they *do* so, or that they *ought* to do so? As to what he calls " the *principle*," that is an inference of *his own*, and not deducible from any thing we said, except by the same means which have distinguished his inferences on many other occasions.

"What is the consequence which must be expected from teaching an illiterate assembly *that the principal design of their union is to extend the practice of a particular ceremony*, but to invest it with an undue importance in their eyes, and by tempting them to look upon themselves as christians of a higher order, to foster an overweening self conceit," &c. (*p.* 258.) If Mr. Hall means that this is the inference from any thing we have said, all that is necessary is to *deny* it; for if we are not to state our sentiments, nor to point out the connection which they have with the different parts of the christian system, without being exposed to such a charge as this, the next step will be, that we must not state our opinions at all:—and if he means to charge this inference on those members of the denomination who are averse to his sentiments, in the consciousness that it is altogether unfounded, they will not think the imputation worthy a detailed refutation.

We are called upon to reflect "on the enormous impropriety of" various things, and among the rest, "of investing every *little Baptist teacher* with the prerogative of repelling from his communion a Howe, a Leighton, or a Brainerd, whom the Lord of glory will welcome to his presence:" and we are then told, that "transubstantiation presents nothing more revolting to the dictates of common sense." (*p.* 265.) This passage strongly shews the contempt in which Mr. Hall holds *little Baptist teachers,* and informs *them* with how much scorn he thinks fit to treat them. We need not turn their apologists. It would be easy to shew, how important are their labours, and how much our denomination owes to their faithful and unwearied exertions; but it is needless. The least of these *little Baptist teachers* who is serving his Lord with humility of mind, has an advocate who will plead his cause, and prove that those who have treated him as if he deserved nothing but to be trampled upon and despised—might, to say the least, have found better employment.

Besides, suppose these *little* Baptist teachers are as *little* as Mr. Hall's degrading expressions represent them, have they forfeited the prerogative of judging for themselves, and of acting on what they conceive the plain directions of God's word? Are they not to venture an opinion, or to act on their convictions in the presence, or in opposition to the wishes of Howe, Leighton, and Brainerd? But even these men with all their excellencies, whatever they were, would not have given the objects of Mr. Hall's scorn any trouble, for we know of no evidence that any of them adopted *his* sentiments, or ever thought either of receiving persons whom they declared not baptised, or of soliciting communion with any who would tell them their own baptism was no better than a *nullity.*

Some assertions are too extravagant to have any other

effect than to secure their own rejection; of this nature is the preceding, that "transubstantiation presents nothing more revolting to the dictates of common sense", than the system which we have advocated. Whoever *knows* what the doctrine of transubstantiation is, and will continue to repeat such an assertion, will probably meet with none who will controvert his position, or endeavour to convince him that he is wrong. A charge which occurs a little before is not much better, that we are "pretending to render a christian society more sacred, and more difficult of access, than the abode of the divine majesty." (*p.* 265.) To this, however, and to every attack of a similar kind, we reply in the words of our author, "peace should be anxiously sought, but always in subordination to purity, and therefore every attempt to reconcile the differences among christians which involves the *sacrifice of truth*, or the least deliberate deviation from the revealed will of Christ, is *spurious* in its *origin*, and *dangerous* in its *tendency*." (*Terms of Com. p.* 5.) Such was his statement on a former occasion. But if Christ made an "inclosure," and left it on record that it was designed to stand through the whole period of his dispensation, why we should deviate from his "revealed will" by removing it, we know not. Nor have we heard any satisfactory reasons why we ought not to raise again the ancient inclosure where it had been thrown down, and to build it exactly in the place in which it formerly stood, in reliance on his wisdom who is the great architect of his church.

"The reader is requested to remember the *extraordinary* positions which Mr. Kinghorn has been compelled to advance in defence of his restrictive system." (*p.* 268.) A list then follows, given in Mr. Hall's usual manner. In our turn we request the reader to remember, that not one of these positions have we ever advanced. They are so garbled and misrepresented, that we entirely disown them, and leave our author to answer for them.

They have in general been examined in the preceding pages, and the observations already made we commit to the reader's consideration.

Mr. Hall "trusts" that a "discerning public" will be convinced that no attempt has been made to evade the force of his opponent's arguments. (*p.* 278.) It is not for us to say what a "discerning public" may think, but a part of that "public" are *Baptists,* and they have discernment enough to see the manner in which he has treated the denomination to which they belong.

No opinion can be ultimately permanent which is not the obvious impression of the New Testament. To support our author's theory it should be proved, that our general sentiment and practice are a misinterpretation of its language and its facts. But if, after all that can be said against us, it is clearly seen that we do no more than the Lord commanded and the Apostles practised, the reproaches of which our author is so profuse, will only sour the minds of some, and convince others that we are right, for they will immediately conclude that such language would not have been used but in the absence of scriptural argument. MR. BAXTER, in his *Infant Church-membership and Baptism,* (*p.* 24,) having briefly stated the evidence in support of the position, that " all that must be admitted visible members must be baptised"; forcibly adds, "I know not what in any shew of reason can be said to this, by those that renounce not scripture. For what man dare go *in a way which hath neither precept nor example to warrant it, from a way that hath a full current of both?* Yet they that will admit members into the visible church without baptism, do so." Again, in reply to the objection, that members "must be baptised after they are stated in the church, (and that many years, as they would have it) I answer, shew *any scripture for that if you can. It is contrary to all scripture example.*" Such plain and open appeals direct the mind at once to the only authority that can decide the controversy.

We are continually urged with the consideration, that our sentiments are opposed to the unity of the church, and our present defence will be accused of tending to increase the spirit of division. Yet sincerely as we lament every thing which occasions painful feeling in the family of God, still divisions themselves are less evils than that unity which arises from the sacrifice of truth. We seek unity by endeavouring to call the attention of men to primitive christianity. Mr. Hall proposes the same end, by discarding what the great body of christians has always believed to be a part of the will of Christ. We acknowledge this is *one method* of promoting unity, which might be applied to an endless variety of cases; since it is difficult to say, what difference might not be cashiered in the same way. For if the direct injunctions of the Lord can be set aside, what may not be given up on the same principle? But one thing is evident; it is not unity alone that is a blessing of such high consequence; no society was more united than the Roman Catholic church during her long reign over the nations; but at no period was either the world or the church in such an awful condition. The unity for which Cyprian contended, and which Mr. Hall praises so highly, was continued in the Romish hierarchy, and extended over the whole western world; but instead of being a blessing, its influence was of the most baneful kind. The only unity worth seeking arises from being of the same mind with Jesus Christ. The declarations of the gospel are simple and plain, and they are summed up by our Lord himself in—faith—baptism—and obedience to what he has commanded. In the present inquiry we have not had to contend for *minutiæ* which we supposed were concealed in the general expression, *all things whatsoever I have commanded you*, and which, it might be said, were open to endless debate; we have had to call the reader's attention to an ordinance expressly named by the Lord himself, and which was the only visible institution he thought proper to specify in his commission. Singular as it may appear to some persons, whoever admits that the commission contains the principles which the christian church should recognise, always places himself on the ground which we have been maintaining. He may differ from us; he may apply sprinkling to infants and call it baptism; if he does, all we ask is, that he would allow us to differ from him. But while he makes the commission his guide, whenever we come in controversy with him, the point of difference relates to the meaning of the injunction, and the interpretation it receives in the conduct of the Apostles, but not to the situation in which it is placed, and its consequent priority to communion. Mr. Hall pursues a different course; he grants our interpretation of the command of Christ respecting the first christian ordinance, he allows that all the facts of the New Testament agree with our interpretation, and that in primitive times they agree also with our system on the subject of communion; yet he contends that persons unbaptised have *now* a *right* to a place in the church, and that we are doing them great injustice to dispute it. If, however, any of his reasonings establish that *right* in the face of such directions and such facts as exist in the New Testament, it is not easy to say where they will stop. But if the sacred volume is to be our rule, our duty is plain, we must *ask for the old paths, where is the good way, and walk therein*. We know we shall have to bear the reproaches of many on this account, but we shall more promote the cause of Christ in the end, by acting in conformity to his primitive appointment, than by adopting maxims, the first operation of which is to *amputate* one of his positive ordinances. In the history of the church we have seen the mischief arising from a corruption of the institutions of the Gospel, and we ought to take warning from former times. The deviations of the early ages were occasioned by one class of assumptions, and the system of Mr. Hall is derived from another, but both *are,* in our esteem, *deviations* from the word of Christ; and to him who travels with the New Testament as his guide, it signifies nothing from whence they originate. His business is to keep in the path trodden by primitive Saints, holy Apostles, and the Son of God; and to remember the admonition, *Wherefore seeing we are also compassed about with so great a cloud of witnesses, let us lay aside every weight, and the sin which doth so easily beset us, and let us run with patience the race set before us, looking unto Jesus the author and finisher of our faith, who, for the joy set before him, endured the cross, despising the shame, and is set down on the right hand of the throne of God. For consider him that endured such contradiction of sinners against himself, lest ye be wearied and faint in your minds. (Heb. xii. 1—3.)*

THE END.

A
Biographical Sketch
of
Joseph Kinghorn
(1766-1932)

by
John Franklin Jones

A
Biographical Sketch
of
Joseph Kinghorn
(1766-1932)

Joseph Kinghorn was born January 17, 1766 at Gateshead, Co. Durham, England to David Kinghorn and was the eldest son of his second wife, Elizabeth. The elder Kinghorn was a shoemaker-became-Baptist-minister in rural Yorkshire and baptized Joseph when the boy was seventeen *(DEB)*.

Classically educated, Joseph was apprenticed to a watchmaker in Hull and, later, to clerk in white- lead works in Newcastle-upon-Tyne. He trained for the ministry at Bristol College and ministered briefly at Fairford, Gloucestershire. Considered by some as too low in his Calvinism, he removed to Norwich *(DEB)*.

Ordained at Norwich in May 1790, he served there from 1789 till his death. The church prospered to point of requiring new construction, and Kinghorn started a new church in Aylsham *(DEB)*.

Kinghorn questioned the ethics of believers taking up arms and consequently, was active in repealing the Test and Corporation Acts. He took wardship of the eight-year-old son of a friend, W. W. Wilkin, even though he himself was a bachelor *(DEB)*.

A Greek, Latin, and Hebrew scholar, he first completed reading the Hebrew Old Testament daily in 1796. He managed a school in his ward and trained young ministers.

He was an avid reader; a skilled preacher; and a member of the Speculative Society, a discussion group consisted mainly of Unitarians *(DEB)*.

He declined the presidency of Northern Education Society's new academy in Bradford (1804) and the principalship of the new Stepney College (1809) *(DEB)*.

He embraced Calvinistic theology, but rejected the Hyper-Calvinist opposition to reasoning with, exhorting, or beseeching sinners to turn to the Lord. He had cordial relations with Arminians and early argued for mixed communion. Reversing his position on the subject, he controverted with Robert Hall over open/mixed communion, advocating the closed position *(DEB)*.

He contributed a critique of a Hebrew New Testament and opposed the circulation of Apocrypha with the biblical text by the Bible Society. Kinghorn was appealed to as an authority in Carey's controversy over using "immerse" for Greek "baptize." He contributed to the BMS, served on its committee, and traveled on its behalf *(DEB)*.

He authored *Baptism, A Term of Communion* (1816) and frequently contributed to *The Baptist Magazine*, the *Eclectic Review*, and the *Evangelical Magazine (DEB)*.

Kinghorn died unmarried September 1, 1832, Norwich, Norfolk, England *(DEB)*.

BIBLIOGRAPHY

Dictionary of Evangelical Biography, 1730-1860. S.v. "Kinghorn, Joseph" by John H. Y. Briggs.

Dictionary of National Biography. S.v. "Kinghorn, Joseph" by Alexander Gordon.

A BIOGRAPHICAL SKETCH OF JOSEPH KINGHORN

Kinghorn, Joseph. *Baptism, A Term of Communion*. Norwich: Bacon, Kinnerbrook & Co., 1816.

BY JOHN FRANKLIN JONES
CORDOVA, TENNESSEE
JUNE 2006

THE BAPTIST STANDARD BEARER, INC.

a non-profit, tax-exempt corporation
committed to the Publication & Preservation
of the Baptist Heritage.

CURRENT TITLES AVAILABLE IN
THE BAPTIST *DISTINCTIVES* SERIES

KIFFIN, WILLIAM A Sober Discourse of Right to Church-Communion. Wherein is proved by Scripture, the Example of the Primitive Times, and the Practice of All that have Professed the Christian Religion: That no Unbaptized person may be Regularly admitted to the Lord's Supper. (London: George Larkin, 1681).

KINGHORN, JOSEPH Baptism, A Term of Communion. (Norwich: Bacon, Kinnebrook, and Co., 1816)

KINGHORN, JOSEPH A Defense of "Baptism, A Term of Communion". In Answer To Robert Hall's Reply. (Norwich: Wilkin and Youngman, 1820).

GILL, JOHN Gospel Baptism. A Collection of Sermons, Tracts, etc., on Scriptural Authority, the Nature of the New Testament Church and the Ordinance of Baptism by John Gill. (Paris, AR: The Baptist Standard Bearer, Inc., 2006).

CARSON, ALEXANDER	Ecclesiastical Polity of the New Testament. (Dublin: William Carson, 1856).
BOOTH, ABRAHAM	A Defense of the Baptists. A Declaration and Vindication of Three Historically Distinctive Baptist Principles. Compiled and Set Forth in the Republication of Three Books. Revised edition. (Paris, AR: The Baptist Standard Bearer, Inc., 2006).
BOOTH, ABRAHAM	Paedobaptism Examined on the Principles, Concessions, and Reasonings of the Most Learned Paedobaptists. With Replies to the Arguments and Objections of Dr. Williams and Mr. Peter Edwards. 3 volumes. (London: Ebenezer Palmer, 1829).
CARROLL, B. H.	*Ecclesia* - The Church. With an Appendix. (Louisville: Baptist Book Concern, 1903).
CHRISTIAN, JOHN T.	Immersion, The Act of Christian Baptism. (Louisville: Baptist Book Concern, 1891).
FROST, J. M.	Pedobaptism: Is It From Heaven Or Of Men? (Philadelphia: American Baptist Publication Society, 1875).
FULLER, RICHARD	Baptism, and the Terms of Communion; An Argument. (Charleston, SC: Southern Baptist Publication Society, 1854).
GRAVES, J. R.	Tri-Lemma: or, Death By Three Horns. The Presbyterian General Assembly Not Able To Decide This Question: "Is Baptism In The Romish Church Valid?" 1st Edition.

	(Nashville: Southwestern Publishing House, 1861).
MELL, P.H.	Baptism In Its Mode and Subjects. (Charleston, SC: Southern Baptist Publications Society, 1853).
JETER, JEREMIAH B.	Baptist Principles Reset. Consisting of Articles on Distinctive Baptist Principles by Various Authors. With an Appendix. (Richmond: The Religious Herald Co., 1902).
PENDLETON, J.M.	Distinctive Principles of Baptists. (Philadelphia: American Baptist Publication Society, 1882).
THOMAS, JESSE B.	The Church and the Kingdom. A New Testament Study. (Louisville: Baptist Book Concern, 1914).
WALLER, JOHN L.	Open Communion Shown to be Unscriptural & Deleterious. With an introductory essay by Dr. D. R. Campbell and an Appendix. (Louisville: Baptist Book Concern, 1859).

For a complete list of current authors/titles, visit our internet site at:
www.standardbearer.org
or write us at:

he Baptist Standard Bearer, Inc.

NUMBER ONE IRON OAKS DRIVE • PARIS, ARKANSAS 72855

TEL # 479-963-3831 *FAX # 479-963-8083*
EMAIL: Baptist@centurytel.net *http://www.standardbearer.org*

Thou hast given a standard to them that fear thee; that it may be displayed because of the truth. — Psalm 60:4

www.ingramcontent.com/pod-product-compliance
Lightning Source LLC
Chambersburg PA
CBHW020752160426
43192CB00006B/319